THE STATE
IS
OUT OF DATE

Praise for *The State is Out of Date*

"*Gregory Sams'* The State is Out of Date *is a book of immense importance that also happens to be immensely readable. Get it now, read it now. You'll be amazed, impressed, persuaded, infuriated and filled with hope for a future that awaits us if only we are prepared to make the right choices. The State IS out of date. We all know it. Now here's the proof and the route map that gets us out of this mess.*"

—GRAHAM HANCOCK, author of *Fingerprints of the Gods*

"*Author Gregory Sams is a prophet of conscience sorely needed at this time to help us swing our compass and set us on the road to sanity once again. He sees the world clearly, uniquely, lovingly—and yet his pen is sharp and cleaves the BS asunder. Get this book and see the world and the way it's working (or rather, not working) and come away with a new ability to describe what you see and despair of. Sams is refreshingly free of clichés and tired old canards. Look at the chapter titles—and you will know the sharpness and aptness of his sword.*"

—LANNY COTLER, film writer and director

"*This is a sarcastically humorous and at times brutally honest overview on many of the problems and divisions that we presently endure through our political and cultural divide. I can't claim that the 'fixes' the author suggests will all work, but he adds some new and fresh perspective to the debate. For those of you who are not especially fond of books on politics, this book is refreshingly easy to follow. How you interpret the result is for each one to individually determine.*"

—ROBERT STEVEN THOMAS, author of *Intelligent Intervention*

THE STATE
IS
OUT OF DATE

We can do it better

Gregory Sams

disinformation®

Published by Disinformation Books, an imprint of
Red Wheel/Weiser, LLC
With offices at
665 Third Street, Suite 400
San Francisco, CA 94107
www.redwheelweiser.com

ISBN: 978-1-938875-06-9

Library of Congress Cataloging-in-Publication Data available upon request

Cover design by Jim Warner
Cover photographs: capital building © Slobodan Djajic/Shutterstock
flowers © Eva105/Shutterstock
Typeset by Maureen Forys, Happenstance Type-O-Rama
Typeset in Warnock Pro with Whitney

EBM
Printed on acid-free paper in the United States of America.

10 9 8 7 6 5 4 3 2 1

Disinformation® is a registered trademark of The Disinformation Company Ltd.

The paper used in this publication meets the minimum requirements of the
American National Standard for Information Sciences-Permanence of Paper for
Printed Library Materials Z39.48-1992 (R1997).

Contents

Peace, A Natural State

Perhaps the sentiments contained in the following pages are not yet sufficiently fashionable to procure them general favor; a long habit of not thinking a thing wrong, gives it a superficial appearance of being right, and raises at first a formidable outcry in defence of custom. But the tumult soon subsides. Time makes more converts than reason.

Thomas Paine's introduction to *Common Sense*, 1776

Slavery was thought normal throughout the world until recent centuries; sex between men and boys was okay with ancient Greeks; for centuries it was tradition to bind women's feet in China; for two thousand years we thought the whole Universe rotated around planet Earth; for more than two centuries we have believed that democratic politics could make big government serve its citizens. Once a belief or practice endures through enough generations it is endowed with the validity of tradition and considered normal. Our trusting response to traditional practice is like the naive belief of young children that adults must know what they are doing, simply because they have been doing it for so long. Even something as bizarre as war is considered normal behavior simply because, after a few thousand years, it has assumed the cloak of tradition.

As a young boy growing up in the wake of World War II, I remember thinking it perfectly plausible that if one person could bring about a great World War, as Hitler had recently done, then it must be possible for one person to bring about a great World Peace. I know better now.

Zoroaster, Jesus, the Buddha, Mohammed, and other prophets and interpreters of spiritual truth have given us some great pointers to inner peace, but the religions that organized after they died have not brought peace and brotherhood to mankind. Indeed, the Abrahamic three have caused a great deal of strife, squabbling over details of just what their same God said to Whom, while believing that if we all followed their chosen version of His word, only then would we achieve global peace and harmony. But people are different, times change, and morality is best developed from within.

Like many, I hoped that some inspired leader, political or spiritual, would come along to get the ball rolling in the right direction and unite us all behind their positive policies. Perhaps a combination of Christ, Gandhi, John Kennedy, and Hypatia of Alexandria would do the trick, provided this composite character could live forever. In despair of this miracle ever arising on Earth, some even anticipate imminent alien contact with a Ten Commandments type of scenario broadcast simultaneously in all languages to all televisions, cell phones, social networks, and radios across the globe. But would even this, an ultimatum from outer space, do the job?

Eventually I came to recognize that while one person's actions can demonstrably plunge large parts of the world into war and disorder, a state of peace can never be constructed or created by the action of a single person, or a select group. It may come as a surprise to discover that a state of peace is as much the natural condition of our world as is the stability that develops in the natural rainforest. A state of balance and harmony arises as the eventual result of billions of people's activities and interests interacting with each other and the rest of the world in a state of freedom. It is constructed from the bottom up. One person or group of people, by whatever means chosen and however enlightened or inspired, cannot determine the specific route to this state of peace. Yet somewhere in our soul we know that peace is a possible condition—something that our species is capable of achieving, despite our lengthy catalog of failures.

> *Peace is not an absence of war; it is a virtue, a state of mind, a disposition for benevolence, confidence, justice.*
>
> Baruch Spinoza, Dutch philosopher and scientist, 1632–1677

I suggest that it is not a natural condition of being human that we must kill and maim each other in large numbers for quite unnecessary reasons. After meeting thousands of people in travels across different continents, cultures, and subcultures, I have come to realize that the vast majority of humanity is not made up of natural-born killers, or even all that evil. In fact, people are great!

Our incessant attempts to forcibly put order into the chaotic and constantly changing mix of our civilization are the reason, I suggest, that we experience so much disorder, suffering, and what is often referred to as "chaos." For too long society has been run with the belief that we are actually able to govern and control something so complex by setting ever more complicated rules and regulations. Wherever this occurs, feedback loops are broken and society's ability to respond and evolve successfully in a changing world is artificially obstructed.

This book is not about some dramatic new way to run the world, according to a plan that seems to make a lot of sense and pushes all your buttons. The world can look after itself and support human beings, as it does every other life form on the planet, if we work within its basic operating framework, which is a fundamentally free system. We perversely refuse to allow big systems the freedom to self-organize, with some thinking the perfect system will arise once they achieve control tantamount to tuning each flap of the proverbial butterfly's wing. We ignore the underlying lesson of the science called chaos theory, which explores the self-organizing powers of complex systems. This arrogant and ignorant behavior by a dominant species threatens not only our own future but perhaps that of the planet itself.

There is a way not to run the planet, and it might seem self-evident that the way it is being done today is a good example. Nevertheless, the usual approach to this situation is to assume that a change of figurehead or a radical re-arrangement of the knobs and levers of power will eventually sort things out. These pages will seek to convince you that no new combination or rearrangement of the complex controls of coercive power will work. Consider the number of states there are in the world, each run by people who believe they know what they are doing, and each tweaked to its local circumstances. Now consider the minor and major tweaking that has gone on throughout the history of the state (pharaoh, senate, church, caliph, king, emperor, prince, president, pope, military junta, parliament, dictator, etc.). There have already been many thousands of different variations and combinations attempted. None of them have worked in the long term, though some may have lasted for longer than others. Do we really believe that, for instance, version 26,733 is going to be the one that finally gets it all working smoothly and sustainably?

Each time that a new government or state takes over the reins of power, we are assured they have the right policies and programs to get the economy back on track, or at least to improve upon the existing situation. And when their programs collapse or fail, they are always most adept at placing the blame elsewhere. I will seek to convince you that there are far too many elements involved in the complex system we call civilization for any single person or group of people to determine its course with coercively backed regulations, made either locally or globally, made with good intent or bad.

The state does perform functions that are necessary to society. It claims the monopoly on these vital functions and does an increasingly poor job of them. We can see crime proliferating as more and more money is spent combating it, while illegal wars and the LIBOR banking fraud of 2012 do not even figure in the crime figures. We see our true health and vitality decline as more and more is spent on sickness care by the state. The widespread notion that more hospital beds and doctors are the sign of a successful "health policy" is truly the sign of a sick nation. In education, agriculture, the roads, social security, medicine and healing, power generation—wherever we look, the determined hand of the state can be seen to degrade and distort that which it seeks to manage and improve.

My proposition is that the means to deal with vital functions can and eventually will arise in a freely operating society so that, for example, robbers, murderers, and identity thieves do not run amok, polluters do not have a free license to destroy our environment, nor spammers to pollute our mailbox. While we need mechanisms to deal with these areas, it is apparent that where we rely upon the state to be that mechanism, it is proving inadequate.

A free society would have no difficulty with many things now thought to be unacceptable by the state. It could tolerate and naturally regulate herbalists, street traders, gambling clubs (we live with the Lottery), prostitution, recreational drug use, and many forms of activity and enterprise now banned or strictly controlled. Much of what consenting adults do with their own bodies and minds, in their own time, is still regulated by criminal law. Alternative medicines are suppressed or banned in some major nations, and many countries still jail homosexuals, or those who dare to question the prevailing government or religion. Yes, we need to manage and regulate some aspects of our culture and develop non-coercive means to do so that are more effective than big government with its growing volume of regulators, inspectors, judges, police, prosecutors, and prisons.

The state's priorities will not change. As we will see, self-interest, self-survival, and self-advancement will always be the primary concerns of any ruler or government. In a democracy, the next election will always be the politician's foremost consideration, and the short-term interests of society will take a poor second best, with our long-term interests hardly considered. When a government is said to be "in power," it holds that power for the simple reason that it is able to make us do or not do that which it decides is in our best, or its best, interest. Whether this power was won in a political bun fight or acquired through military force often makes little difference in the long run. Once a new state is seen to have a firm grip upon the reins of power, the world will recognize it and welcome it to the family of nations.

There are more questions than answers in this book. This is not a pessimistic view, but one based on the premise that our current methods of attacking the problems of the world actually block the emergence of organic working solutions. Nor will every aspect of every subject be aired, or copious examples delivered on every principle. The intention is to stir the pot rather than draft a finished recipe with measured ingredients. If I were to cite evidence supporting each point or assertion, then many of these chapters would fill a book of their own.. You can view this book as a jigsaw puzzle with a few of the pieces missing. The picture is there, and as you see it, you will be in a better position to fill in the missing pieces yourself.

Everything that is really great and inspiring is created by the individual who can labor in freedom.

Albert Einstein, theoretical physicist, 1879–1955

1

What Would an Alien Think?

Imagine for a moment that you are an intelligent alien on your first visit to planet Earth, coming from a planet as richly developed as ours, but with freedom, instead of top-down state control, underpinning its culture. Your alien civilization may have little in common with Earth's, but could include any of the things we enjoy, such as music, dance, literature, sports, architecture, engineering, science, art, fashion, and so on. After all, none of these things were conceived, planned, or developed by the state, though at times it may seek to regulate some of them for the declared benefit of us all.

Most people today would assume that this alien must have a central commander and head of state. They assume this because central command is all that we have in our own limited frame of reference, and is the stuff of a million science fiction stories.

Central command is certainly NOT the natural state. We have only to look around us to realize that every other life form sharing this planet has operated successfully for millennia without any form of central controlling structure. The dinosaurs dominated for thirty-five times the period that we have been on the planet, as far as we know without the need of parliaments, kings, or ruling bodies.

I know of no voting council of trees which determines the specific proportions and varieties of trees in a given forest. In many cases, such as the oak tree, the long-term successful species has figured out how to cooperate with as many other species as possible (up to three hundred, in the case of the oak). This ability to cooperate with other forms of life is a far more intelligent long-term survival strategy than is that of domination and control by rulers and ruling bodies.

Why do we assume that any intelligent alien species, even more advanced than ours, will have the same sort of flawed structures as ourselves, with powerful leaders, military forces, and lawmaking bodies? Why is it inconceivable to us that any other advanced civilization could be operating, as does every successful structure in the Universe, in a state of freedom? These aren't deep questions—they just reveal the deep rut in which our imagination is trapped.

We assume that any intelligent creature capable of space travel will come equipped with plasma guns, ionic blasters, phaser bolts, and a full arsenal of high-tech weaponry with which to kill and destroy. Why? We humans have experienced a dramatic and possibly unique evolution of methods to kill each other. A mainstay of our chosen cultural entertainment involves depictions of us killing each other in countless war and confrontational movies. Are we to assume that this is a normal or natural element of any highly developed civilization?

> *Is mankind alone in the Universe? Or are there somewhere other intelligent beings looking up into their night sky from very different worlds and asking the same kind of question?*
>
> Carl Sagan and Frank Drake

Our alien may have learned how to travel along the fractal patterns of hyperspace and be able to outmaneuver a missile or fighter jet. But it is quite possible that its civilization never figured out how to split the atom. Maybe it never had the fear of a Hitler to inspire its scientists to tap such a destructive force. The consequences of this discovery have been extremely negative and continue to pose an ongoing threat to the very survival of our species. Yet we assume that a higher alien intelligence will have even greater means of self-destruction at its disposal. This is a basically illogical assumption. More destructive power is neither the hallmark of higher intelligence nor the route to long-term peace and stability.

We assume that our highly developed alien will have a highly developed state overseeing a well-regulated society. Yet what does the central controlling state actually give us—not one specific state here or there, but the beast in general— the totality of states running their own big and little nations throughout the world? They primarily came into being for one reason alone—to protect us from other versions of themselves. It is difficult to find anything else they do that we treasure, or are satisfied by. They take vast sums of money from us and send back a little here and there, sprinkling it on the poor and hungry if they are left-wing, or subsidizing the unworthy and unnecessary if they are right-wing. The majority of it though, whichever wing of the bird the center tilts toward, is wasted and squandered in useless, unproductive, and often downright damaging activities.

Probably 80 percent of what the state does is unnecessary or unproductive, things we are quite capable of sorting out in society without resorting to one ruling body, supported by police, the military, nuclear arsenals, parliaments, dictators, presidents, and vast armies of bureaucrats. I refer to things such as which side of the road we drive on, what size food packaging must be, how we generate electricity, what constitutes an acceptable dwelling or house, how two people make a commitment to each other, what types of medicine we use, or how many hours we work in a week. Don't imagine that we would live in some disordered mess without a central command issuing all these rules. Wherever they do not exist in our society we seem to have developed real order.

The other 20 percent of the state's frame of activities consists of valuable and necessary governing functions. Unfortunately, the state often delivers inadequate and wasteful services in these areas—services that are deteriorating rather than improving. These vital functions vary from state to state, but usually include some mix of essential areas such as education, roads, healthcare, power, crime, safety regulation, aid and charity, transportation, or the press. Where the state does not directly govern these areas, it often seeks to regulate them and exert influence upon them.

So what happened to our imaginary alien? Well, I hope that he or she will spend enough time to feel a sense of awe for the beauty of this planet and for many of the wonderful technological and cultural achievements arising from our own unique evolution through the chaos of society. But, if our alien is intelligent, recognize that planet Earth is a dangerous place for its own massively armed human inhabitants, let alone a relatively peaceful creature visiting from another world.

We can understand why our visitor might have reticence about "coming out" in our civilization, and want to "hyperspace" it back to a civilization whose free inhabitants had long ago found peace and stability, without the need to forcibly control and kill each other in its pursuit. They will also, perhaps, have found ways to do this without disrespecting and degrading the ecosystem that supports them. And I think it unlikely that our alien would willingly choose to share the secrets of space travel with us.

Disclaimer: *Readers are advised not to accept lifts in any unidentified spaceships. The author has no idea who or what is "out there" and simply uses "our alien" as a vehicle for taking a different perspective of our own system—and to discourage the assumption that the way we Earthlings run society is a natural thing.*

2

The Emperor Has No Clothes

We shall get nowhere until we start by recognising that political behavior is largely non-rational, that the world is suffering from some kind of mental disease which must be diagnosed before it can be cured.

George Orwell, 1903–1950

We all know the story of the little boy who not only realized that the emperor was wearing no clothes, but also acknowledged that he saw it, and said so, even though everybody else was acting exactly as if the emperor did have his clothes on. Today it is apparent that the state has lost any of the merit that we imagine it had in "the old days." Deep inside, more and more of us realize that our structure of government is a decaying system; all over the world, we read daily of its latest dire activities against our civilization and of past abuses now revealed. Ever more eyes are opening.

Today the term "for political reasons" is commonly taken to mean that something is not being done for genuine reasons. In this sense, our own linguistic "body language" tells us what we really think of politics. Politicians rate below every other group in numerous surveys that gauge public respect for different professions. The 2011 Transparency International Survey found that worldwide, 80 percent of people regard political parties as corrupt institutions. By this time "Occupy" movements were springing up across the world as people protested the iniquity of big government joined at the hip to big business, treating us as consumers who must be stimulated to continually buy more.

In today's age most of us have greater confidence in our bicycle repair shop, plumber, or the local supermarket than we do in our government (those who profess to be supplying us with the essential need of running our society and protecting our borders). It is sobering to recognize that few of those who claim the right to run our country would be able to successfully manage a small business in the marketplace they have distorted to favor the corporate chains and multinationals. Few of us can look into our souls and really believe that the state is working.

> *Government is not reason. Government is not eloquence. It is force. And, like fire, it is a dangerous servant and a fearful master.*
>
> George Washington, first US President, 1732–1799

Yet most of us go about our daily lives acting as though the emperor does indeed have on his new clothes, heatedly comparing one politician's outfit with another's. We earnestly wish they would "do something effective" about this or that problem, bemoaning the hundreds of billions wasted on shelved missile projects, bank bailouts, and failed employment schemes—thinking that some new leader with a radical new plan is going to stop it from happening.

We refuse to openly recognize that the emperor has no clothes because the alternatives seem so horrific. If the emperor really is naked, then

- Who will run the emergency wards?

- Who will pay the unemployed?

- Who will maintain employment in the arms industry?

- Who will keep our streets safe?

- Who will make sure our air is not poisonous?

- Who will safeguard the farming industry?

- Who will educate our children?

- Who will insure the nuclear power industry?

- Who will ensure that our banking system is sound?

- Who will decide what foods and drugs are safe?

- Who will look after us when we cannot look after ourselves?

These may be important and vital issues, but the size of the issue and the need for action should not blind us to the obvious. The archaic/modern state cannot sustainably deliver what it promises when it moves in to control these vital issues. This seems to be the case whether we are talking about Uncle Sam, the Taliban, the former Soviet Union, or present-day Russia. I would be interested to hear of those countries in the world where, in private, a majority of the inhabitants are genuinely satisfied with their government's efforts. There would be a few, I hope.

Of course, so many of the terrible problems that we depend on governments around the world to deal with are caused by governments around the world. It is the state in general, our protecting emperor, that carries out, sanctions, or aggravates the activities that create terrorists, orphans, refugees, wars, the homeless, famines, bankruptcies, bulging jails, unsupported families, the unemployed, and even mad cows, as we shall see. And as the empire approaches bankruptcy, we discover the protecting emperor long ago sold off the entire wardrobe and its contents, including us, now bonded debtors to the banks.

> *Politicians are, in fact, in the business of getting and keeping power and everything else is subordinate to that. As I have grumbled before, there is no such thing as "good government," certainly not in the sense that some businessmen look for it. There is a lot of government and there is a little government. If you are lucky, you get the latter. We are unlucky.*
>
> Andrew Alexander, British journalist, 1997

3

The State Is Out of Date

The budget should be balanced. Public debt should be reduced. The arrogance of officialdom should be tempered, and assistance to foreign lands should be curtailed.

Marcus Tullius Cicero, Rome, 63 BCE

Some writers have so confounded society with government, as to leave little or no distinction between them; whereas they are not only different, but have different origins. Society is produced by our wants, and government by our wickedness; the former promotes our happiness positively by uniting our affections, the latter negatively by restraining our vices. The one encourages intercourse, the other creates distinctions. The first is a patron, the last a punisher.

Thomas Paine, *Common Sense*, 1776

Perhaps there was a time when the state was the lesser of two evils—when it was necessary to have strong men willing to kill on command in order to protect us from the bakers, weavers, farmers, and organized marauders living over the hill or across the waters. In most conflicts then and now, the danger arises out of a confrontation between those who have control over territory and those who seek to wrest it from them, and with it the right to harvest taxes and natural resources. It's been going on for so long now that we could easily be fooled into thinking it has always been this way, with somebody in charge regulating from the top down.

For a few thousand years before the first coercive state appeared we human beings were doing what we're good at—working together and creating value. Whether in networks of villages or in the world's earliest cities, we saw trade, culture, and civilization develop and flourish. The great drivers of this advance were not powerful central states but our harnessing of fire, smelting of metal, understanding of agriculture, and gathering for sacred purposes. The simultaneous shift away from hunting and gathering enabled a massive release of human potential, the basic building block of civilization.

If you ever get to the British Museum, make a point of visiting the Ancient Mesopotamia rooms. There are several of them reaching eight and a half thousand years back to 6500 BCE. I have scoured them twice and not been able to find a single artifact representing weapons, warriors, chariots, or conquest—prior to 2600 BCE. That time marked the first record of organized violence, when a few hundred armed men from Sumer vanquished the Elamites, inaugurating the coercive state. Other cities in the Fertile Crescent soon built armies for protection, and these armies got into fights, as they do. Within a few centuries Sargon of Akkad created an army powerful enough to subjugate twenty other prosperous cities thriving in what is now Iraq, "unifying" them. This was, essentially, organized theft on a grand scale, creating the world's first empire and setting a pattern that persisted.

Wherever it appeared, the coercive state concept spread, often carried by men with swords, or prompted by the fear of them. It eventually reached Rome, where it flourished on the back of slavery and conquest. Roman legionnaires brought it to Britain, from where it was shipped to the American Colonies—arriving over four thousand years after that first war in Sumer. By the end of the last century every patch of land on the planet was under the jurisdiction of one state or another.

Whatever the color of today's coercive state, its foundations and modus operandi have changed little since ancient times, though its reach of responsibility has extended. Whether we are being told what to do by kings, pharaohs, priests, presidents, emperors, generals, senates, or democratically elected representatives, the resultant state operates on the same basic principles of managing its dominion with coercively backed laws. The underlying formula of these laws goes: "Do (or don't do) this or we will damage you." These proclaimed laws should not be confused with natural laws such as those of gravity and thermodynamics—laws that need no legislation, just understanding. Instead of relying upon popular paying support for its public service, the state has traditionally funded itself through methods that rely on its creation of the law and ownership of the police and military. As we will see in the next chapter, these principles of state management are flawed and destined to fail whenever and for whatever purposes they are applied.

Maybe civilization did get a boost from some of the stability that early governing states were able to achieve. We certainly know that rulers today and in the past have always taken credit for the achievements of civilization that occurred during their reign. Yet too often we have seen a large part of that civilization's achievements destroyed with the state when it is eventually conquered or collapses under the weight of its own overgrown bureaucracy. This happened dramatically in the former Soviet Union, which ultimately fell apart under the weight of its own uselessness, without any actual penetration or provocation from outside forces or agencies.

> *In all ages, whatever the form and name of government, be it monarchy, republic, or democracy, an oligarchy lurks behind the façade.*
>
> Ronald Syme, scholar on ancient Rome, 1903–1989

Time and again has the accumulated knowledge of earlier civilizations been lost when their empires were conquered and destroyed. Despite the enduring power of the Egyptian empire, even its language was lost until the Rosetta Stone was discovered in 1799. Great thriving cities such as Carthage and Constantinople were razed. Most of Archimedes' knowledge was lost, along with his life, when the Romans took Syracuse in 212 BCE. The famous Library of Alexandria, greatest storehouse of knowledge in the ancient world, was destroyed by a Christian mob in 391 soon after the Roman Empire officially "converted" to Christianity (it probably contained a room dedicated to pyramid building). When invading Mongols ransacked Baghdad's House of Wisdom in 1258, the Tigris River ran black for three days with the ink of manuscripts and red with the blood of scientists and philosophers. Most of the indigenous knowledge and culture of Africa and the Americas was lost following conquest by European nations between the sixteenth and nineteenth centuries. What little survives today remains under attack. As this writing approached the finish line in 2013, the ancient library at Timbuktu was under attack by militant religious fundamentalists intent on its destruction. It still goes on.

Claims are often made for the civilizing effect of having rulers and empires, citing the patronage of the arts and the ability of an iron hand to keep things stable enough for culture to develop. Yet the world is full of magnificent ruins from civilizations past—the temples, statues, and fortresses surviving as monuments to the pomp and paranoia of rulers past. Had the Iron Age known dynamite, it is unlikely that even these would be left behind. What will remain of our culture in a thousand, or ten thousand years? Will the hard drives of the information age be decipherable?

A government big enough to give you everything you want, is strong enough to take everything you have.

Thomas Jefferson, American Founding Father, 1743–1826

The main reason most of us believe it necessary to have a state of some sort centrally controlling society is because it's been done that way for so long that we cannot imagine there is any other way to do it. How else would we decide where to build new roads, or how to deal with criminals, or what chemicals are safe to include in our food chain? The fact that our road program has gone berserk, that cybercrime proliferates, and that our food chain is polluted with damaging toxins rarely comes to mind when we consider with horror the void that we imagine would be left without "central control" telling us all just what we need to do and making damn sure we do it—or else!

In practice, we can see from history that management of the system by dictate has not worked so far, and now we can see the reason why this is so and recognize that it could never be possible. Yet we are so used to its inefficiencies, iniquities, and regular horrors that we accept it with resignation as the way of the world—thinking it a necessary evil. It does not seem to matter much whether the state is run by good men or bad—or even run by women. It does not seem to matter whether it gets power by divine right, inheritance, struggles for freedom, or democratic elections. When every state comes to its inevitable demise, those elements of society that it has been controlling most are generally those in the greatest disarray. Hospitals seize up, law and order decay, and money for social support runs out.

Yet we still believe that without this system in place there would be a terrible void, gross disorder, and degeneration of society into some kind of a violent and frightening morass ruled by the whim of the mob. In fact, as we shall see, most aspects of a stable society that we can depend on evolved outside of this state-run system.

In contrast, the state's modus operandi is to determine just what is an average standard of living and then try to legislate us all into it, either by supporting people who have not reached the ideal standard, or by penalizing those who choose some other way to live. Why on Earth should we let officials of the government be responsible for our living standards, when so many of the problems they deal with are caused by them or would not be seen as a problem by anyone else but them?

It has been said that democracy is the worst form of government—except all those other forms that have been tried from time to time.

Winston Churchill, 1874–1965

In a sense the state, like slavery or war, has always been a very flawed concept. It doesn't work, has never worked, and is not in the long-term interest of our society, our civilization, or our own personal evolution. That said, it seemed like a reasonable way to run things—especially when everybody else was doing it. But we haven't found a way to make it work in five thousand years and we threaten our very existence with our persistence in putting new clothes on the Emperor. Five thousand years is not a long time in our own evolution on this planet, which has spanned two million years or more, thirty thousand or so of them civilized.

We are now faced with some clear evidence that this system cannot work. The one constant feature binding the states that have been trying to run their territories for four and a half thousand years is the foundation stone of *determinism*. Determinism is, quite simply, the belief that by central planning with the right information one can determine the development and future state of a complex system. It is the belief that by passing man-made laws and launching programs and plans we can more positively affect and effectively control the evolution of society than it can do by itself.

> *What luck it is for governments that the people they rule do not think.*

> Adolf Hitler, 1889–1945

This intent to control, it now seems, is equivalent to believing we could do a better job of managing the solar system by adjusting and carefully regulating the orbits and rotations of each of its planets, moons, and asteroids. What science can do with some success is make a prediction of what a complex system is going to do, or at least guess the probability of various possible outcomes. What it cannot do is alter or accurately influence the outcome of the system by mandate, underwritten with manipulation of some of its parts and punishment for those parts that do not comply.

The new discoveries of science provided by the study of chaotic systems show us not only that efforts to mechanistically control them are futile, but also that they have an organizing force of their own. That is to say that chaotic systems, systems built up from an uncountable number of parts operating independently in an unpredictable manner, have a tendency to organize themselves into stable and flexible working systems, constantly adjusting themselves according to feedback from within and without the system. The information that fuels this process is the continual exchange between all of the system's uncountable components, feeding back information and reaction from one to another. This is portrayed as a system made up of multiple-layered "feedback loops" weaving patterns at all levels throughout—organizing themselves around things called "strange attractors."

A good example of such a system is the rainforest, which creates a stable system sustaining the existence of its myriad components, while delivering oxygen to the rest of the globe as a by-product. Another manifestation of chaos organizing itself is the evolution of music in our society, evolving through constantly new harmonies, forms, and technologies in order to provide continual new variations of pleasure for billions of differently tuned ears.

We could worry much less about the fate of the Amazon rainforest had the Brazilian state not been actively subsidizing its clearance for cattle ranching, as well as building roads and facilities for foreign timber interests. One of the "jokes" in the rainforest is "Where's the beef?" as many contractors simply clear the land, take the money, and run, rather than sticking around for the precarious business of trying to feed cattle on the thin topsoil that is exposed. The state, in its brazen desire to expand its effective tax base, spends great sums of public money to entice business to rape an ecosystem that otherwise would have remained economically untouched. Though the whole project bears all the hallmarks of a disaster that will be forever regretted, it could be doggedly pursued for years by a state that will always have successors to be responsible for its short sightedness.

And just imagine if our society believed music to be so important to our lives that it had to be regulated, like housing, with strict government controls and regulation. Would we ever have had jazz, rhythm & blues, rock 'n roll, the Beatles, punk rock, acid house, psytrance, ambient music, or techno in any of its growing manifestations? The state of the music industry in France today is a testament to that government's absurd attempts to legislate the content of music in order to maintain its French "cultural integrity." The French government has at least excluded classical music from its complex regulations; unfortunately, many of the great dead composers were not French, a situation which even the French government recognizes to be unalterable.

That the state is unable to deterministically manage a system as complex as human society is evident in every such area over which they exert control. A classic case in Europe is the Common Agricultural Policy which, through trying to safeguard our food supply, has come to pose the greatest threat both to European farming and to our health.

Some effects of the Common Agricultural Policy are

- It counters our evolutionary change to a healthier diet, by interfering with the essential and effective feedback loop supplying information from the consumer to the producer. Subsidizing farmers and producing according to central decision making interferes negatively with the natural information exchange. The Soviets tried to do it and failed.

- It encourages the introduction of toxic chemicals to our ecosystem through supporting and subsidizing food production beyond society's demands. Much of the use of toxic chemicals and treatments is, when not mandated, certainly encouraged by the state's guarantee to purchase or subsidize the sale. This overrides the natural feedback loop between farmer and consumer, thereby lowering the quality of our food.

- It is responsible for the surplus of cattle that were fed back to themselves, as a means of reducing the "beef mountain." This created the conditions for the growth and spread of BSE (Mad Cow Disease). The original cause of this modern tragedy is the intervention of the state in our food chain. The main alternative theory, put forward by organic farmer Mark Purdey, points to the effects of a state-imposed painting of all British cattle with a highly toxic organo-chloride potion covering the head and spinal column.

- It has been cited by regular studies as unworkable, corruption-prone, and grossly inefficient since the early 1980s. Literally billions of euros, taken from the pockets of the European populace, are scammed and lost every year as this out-of-control creation of Brussels gets on with its regular job—which itself has little merit.

Yet somewhere in Brussels, nerve center of the faltering European Union, the wielders of deterministic power think that even more of our money and some clever manipulation of their ever more complex formulae will get it all working. The alternative of lost jobs (their own) and responsibilities is too awful to contemplate. As I upgrade this book from 1998 to 2013 it looks like perhaps the end is nigh for the European Union, an unnecessary and costly extra layer of government that never served to reduce levels of local or national government beneath it, providing little more than more pigs feeding at the metaphorical trough.

In the US an equally damaging intervention in the food chain has also brought dire consequences, as agribusiness flourishes upon the subsidies intended to ensure plenty of meat on every American's plate. Government legislation allows GMOs (genetically modified organisms) to enter the food chain without adequate testing or identity labeling, treating the population of the US as guinea pigs in a huge and uncertain experiment. It is disconcerting to know that insurance companies regard GMOs as uninsurable (along with wars and nuclear accidents), leaving the state to assume liability for any damage they may do. Through government subsidy, 40 percent of the US corn crop (2011) is converted to "biofuels," in order to feed cars instead of people, with the conversion estimated to consume 70 percent more fossil fuel energy than the biofuel delivers. Yes, it's madness. The first efforts to introduce natural foods to the US suffered a setback in 1966 when the FBI raided the offices of America's first macrobiotic center, seizing and burning dangerous books that suggested a diet of whole cereals, legumes, and vegetables was more conducive to good health than a diet of hamburgers and french fries washed down with milkshakes and cola drinks.

I leave it to researchers and historians to determine, but suggest that almost any large empire, in the final 10 percent of its term, has more government employees, police, and military in place, managing more volumes of laws and regulation than at any other point in the initial 90 percent of its existence. I suggest that this applies as much to the Aztec Empire as to the Roman Empire, as much to the former Soviet Union as to the world's current surviving superpower. (This paragraph is unchanged from the 1998 edition, when the idea of America ever losing its global number one status was alien to most.)

Corruptissima republica plurimae leges.
The worse the state, the more laws it has.

Tacitus, 55–120 AD

People may plan their lives ahead and often live out the plan successfully; companies can plan five-year strategies and projects that may come to fruition. But in neither instance is civilization as a whole forced to accept these plans, which stand or fall on their own merit. Should someone in Japan develop a car that runs on water, then all the plans of the oil companies will need rapid alteration. We are part of the chaotic mix of billions of entities making decisions that affect all of the other entities on the planet in unpredictable ways—the ways of a complex system. If they do fit in and positively enhance our lives, they survive and prosper.

Our recently discovered appreciation of the nature of complex chaotic systems (see next chapter) gives a clear explanation for the eventual failure of past and future government programs that forcibly manipulate and manage "vital" aspects of the complex system that is our society, and the world in which it is set. In virtually every area that the state controls, the natural feedback loop inherent in a complex system is broken. We cannot expect "our say" at the ballot box to make more than a marginal difference. We know that whoever is in power will be ineffectual and a waste of our money—and yet we continue to avoid even wondering if there are possible alternatives to the palpable madness of the modern state, democratic or otherwise.

In this book we will see that however the controls are rearranged, the state will never be able to legislate the world into peace, harmony, and sustainable progress. It appears to have no positive part to play in the healthy or successful evolution of our species and its own activities are indeed counter-evolutionary. The coercive state does not work and many now realize this, accepting it only as a necessary evil. But there it is—what to do? First of all, stop believing that the state is necessary, stop being frustrated by its inevitable failures, and stop expecting that it will get something right in the long run. By realizing that the state is not a viable option, we open ourselves up to the discovery of alternative forms of managing our society.

> *I think that people want peace so much that one of these days government had better get out of the way and let them have it . . . Every warship, every tank, and every military aircraft built is, in the final sense, a theft from those who are hungry and are not fed, from those who are naked and not clothed.*
>
> Dwight D. Eisenhower, US President, 1890–1969

4

Chaos Theory

Three times in his speech President Bush (the first one) recited that now familiar phrase "new world order."... The trouble is that order is a 19th-century concept. It suggests Metternichian arrangements of large, heavy, somewhat static entities. History in the late 20th century seems to belong more to chaos theory and particle physics and fractals; it moves by bizarre accelerations and illogics, by deconstructions and bursts of light.

Time, March 1991

Most people will ascribe shocking and scary connotations to the word "chaos," often put to good use in newspaper-selling headlines about disorder and disruption. This is not what the science dubbed "chaos theory" is about, and there is not any one theory to it—any more than there is one theory to physics or biology. Chaos theory looks at how a rainforest achieves stability and balance without anybody centrally programming what grows where and when. It shows us that the wild chaos of the rainforest manages to succeed as a harmonious whole with no imposed control unless humans, usually funded by state subsidies, bulldoze it.

Chaos theory defines a new attitude to the world that science studies. It has stimulated many new branches of science, having names like complexity theory, anti-chaos theory, dynamical systems theory, and non-linear dynamics. Working with and understanding chaos theory has led to tools that enable scientists to see the bigger picture, whether they are biologists, geologists, botanists, or sociologists. And it has given mathematicians new ways to describe what is going on in the world around us, and inside us. Scientists had been sliding down a reductionist path, seeking to understand the mechanics of life by looking at ever smaller particles of it. Chaos theory also explains why the synchronicity that so often astounds us in life is, indeed, just another manifestation of the patterned web that connects our Universe together.

This book refers to chaos theory and specifically to the implications it has for our approach to the management of human affairs. However, most of it will ring true to your own experience of life, whether or not science had ever discovered the patterned dynamics that self-organize within a complex system. Though a small library has been written on the multiplying dimensions of this new science, there appear to be few scientists who have looked through its lenses at the way in which we deterministically run our society. Scientists must be wary of lost funding and the potential career damage that can result from straying into areas not traditionally considered to be the province of a serious science.

The most ardent advocates of chaos theory will convincingly explain the linkage between today's hurricane and a butterfly's wing flap in Guatemala six months earlier. Yet few of these scientists would ever consider, for instance, that the location of the sun which holds our planet in orbit, or a moon with the power to lift our mighty oceans, might have any effect upon the development of a delicate fetus. Astrology is a taboo subject for scientists, and has been ever since it was denounced by the Church as occult and declared off limits. Scientists who dismiss astrology as nonsense nevertheless have great respect for legendary astrologers of old, such as Ptolemy and Kepler, whose interest in the spirits of the heavens led them to chart its movements and thus progress the science of astronomy.

"Real" scientists avoid the dangers of getting involved with the vague and illogical areas of social organization and politics. Social science is a dirty word to most pure scientists, and it's not surprising when you consider some of the appalling things that have been done in its name (such as Soviet scientific crime predictions setting mandatory targets for police arrests, and Hitler's quest to breed the perfect Aryan race). Perhaps as a result, there has been little application of this new science to the study of social organization. Yet the light that chaos theory sheds upon the way in which we govern our society ultimately holds the greatest lessons for us all.

The origins of this science, spawned in the 1970s, are briefly explored here, but it is not the purpose of this book to dazzle you with all the implications of its growing usage in image compression, financial forecasting, mineral prospecting, medicine, traffic flow dynamics, data encryption, and the creation of "living" landscapes in the movie *Avatar*. Suffice it to say here that chaos theory has given scientists the tools and understanding needed to see what is happening in a far bigger picture than they could ever see before. The benefits of this are manifest.

The focus of this short book is on us, all of us together, for we are all part of a complex system in which anything affects everything. We will look at the usual world in a different way, forgetting for a moment much of what we have always taken for granted. The human race has not been on this planet nearly long enough for anyone to seriously argue that something must be done a certain way, "because that's the way it has always been done." We have existed as humans for 5 percent of the time span that dinosaurs lived on Earth, and have been experimenting with coercively based social management for less than 5 percent of the time that modern humans have been around. We now have a science that shows why this recent experiment has never provided a sustainable long-term result, a social system that always adapts and never collapses.

There is no $E=mc2$ type of equation to sum up the essence of chaos theory, though the formula most likely to be identified with it is the elegantly simple one that reveals the infinite world of the Mandelbrot set: $Z = z2+c$. The discovery of chaos theory has given science the tools and the inclination to study the overall patterns and form of the subject being studied, with less emphasis on reducing the subject into ever smaller pieces according to the reductionist approach. Believe it or not, science has discovered the concept of the whole!

In pre-Babylonian times Chaos was perceived as the mysterious space between Heaven and Earth, and the source of inspiration, form, and change in this world. Surprisingly, this is closer to today's scientific usage of the word than that it is given in the newspapers. The quantum shift to a deterministic attitude, and the belief that man had dominance over planet Earth, appears to have begun its history around 3000 BCE for most of the emerging civilizations we know about today— our approximate period of recorded history. This shift is classically depicted in the Babylonian myth in which Marduk, symbol of man's control, kills Tiamat, the dragon goddess of Chaos. This is the same Earth dragon spirit that represents the organized forces of nature in the ancient Chinese tradition and many others.

Invention, it must be humbly admitted, does not consist in creating out of void, but out of chaos.

Mary Wollstonecraft Shelley, 1797–1851

Though tribal and pagan religions since ancient times have recognized a more holistic partnership with our planet, the world's three major monotheistic religions have viewed Earth as something over which they claim domain and ownership rights. It was all made by God expressly for humankind's benefit, according to the same Old Testament story to which Jews, Christians, and Muslims subscribe. The legend of St. George killing the symbolic dragon maintains the misguided affirmation that mankind is able to control the chaos and shape culture by force, according to his own preconceived order. As we will see, the power of chaos that we naturally harness to change our world is demonstrated in virtually all of the achievements of civilization and technology that we treasure. Yet where we deterministically force the chaos, as would-be masters of the Earth, the resultant product all too often ends up bringing misery and confusion for our species.

The discovery of chaos theory challenges centuries of deterministic thinking that has infused religion, science, and government. The societies that we form in this world can no longer be viewed as if they are giant and very complicated machines that need a control structure of ever increasing complexity in order to be successfully managed. The secret of nature's most complex structures is in the simple techniques by which they are built and managed from the bottom up, combining repetitive acts with the strangely helpful chaos of unpredictability. The network of nature consists of an infinite number of components acting as feedback loops into the whole. Each component is constantly feeding information and activity into the system and modulating its own behavior according to the whole system's activity. Sometimes the results of this connected network appear magical.

The science of chaos theory has a more holistic view of the world and recognizes the apparently universal tendency of complex systems to create order within themselves—to exhibit what is termed "self-organization." The capacity of the world to create harmony on its own, to create a pattern within a multitude of events, is one that has been glimpsed by mystics and artists from time immemorial. Scientists now recognize it too, and in the next century these new discoveries may join the ranks of relativity and quantum mechanics. Scientists can now witness this harmony of self-organization and recreate it using fractal geometry on a computer—which led to these mathematical fractals being dubbed the "Thumbprint of God."

One must still have chaos in oneself to be able to give birth to a dancing star.

Friedrich Nietzsche, 1844–1900

The mathematical fractal discoveries were a by-product of mathematician Benoit Mandelbrot's determination to discover the geometry of the repetitive patterns that he recognized in nature. This fractal mathematics offered scientists in other fields the tools they needed to see and measure previously unrecognized structures existing in many phenomena. Mandelbrot (1924–2010) was frustrated by the inability of Euclidean geometry to measure natural forms like mountains, clouds, and trees. These features of Earth are made up neither of circles, rectangles, triangles, nor straight lines, yet the Latin roots of "geo-metry" mean measurement of the Earth. Mandelbrot had a particularly perceptive pair of eyes and enjoyed using them and acknowledging their inputs. This is not a very "scientific" thing to do; the human eye, as science's dispassionate observer, was meant to record data, not to make insightful observations. Benoit's eyes recognized the repetitive geometry that made up a tree, a bank of clouds, or a range or mountains. He saw the formula of the clouds before he was able to mathematically describe it with numbers and letters.

It was after starting work on the fractal geometry of nature that Benoit Mandelbrot was led to research the near-abandoned work of two unusual French mathematicians from 1918–1919, Julia and Fatou. He studied the peculiar nonlinear equations they worked with and, in an attempt to map them out, discovered (in 1980) the now famous Mandelbrot set—the strangest beast ever found through mathematics. When you understand fractals, you understand that they are no more generated by the computer than is a photograph generated by the camera. The Mandelbrot set and other fractals exist through the repeatable but unexpected, unpredictable, and inexplicable organization of points on a piece of paper.

The computer simply enables us to see a representation of how these individual points have behaved when struck with a formula. The points are simply those points on the page or computer screen that have been assigned the value of the coordinates of their location were you to make a simple *x,y* line graph of that page. In much the same way that an old film camera will show us how each light beam behaved when it touched the identical grains on the photographic film, neither the computer nor the formula actually creates the fractal image. It is done by the process of iteration, of repeating the same process over and over with a very slight modification each time it is done. That same powerful process is the key to meditation, to chanting of mantras or Hail Marys, and to the moving fractal images that can be derived through manipulating the constant feedback of a video camera to its own starting image.

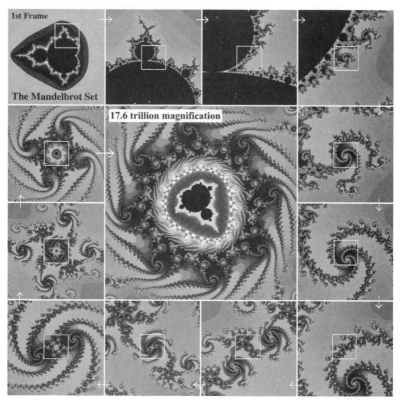

Zoom into the Mandelbrot set—final frame magnification is 17.6 trillion

Scientists now recognize patterns of self-organization in far more exciting areas than the dots on a blank computer screen. They are becoming aware of a Universe composed of interlinking sub- and super-levels of organization such as that which exists within the random neural network of our own brains and within the self-regulating phenomena that keep this Earth's atmosphere within those very narrow and seemingly precarious parameters necessary for life. James Lovelock was the first scientist to recognize our Earth itself as a whole living organism, consisting of infinite interconnected components. Many pre-Abrahamic cultures had an idea of this too, without having explored it in such depth or even thinking it needed putting to the proof.

One of the other great discoveries of chaos theory is that called "sensitive dependence on initial conditions." This is commonly known as the "Butterfly Effect," the recognition by Edward Lorenz that something as insignificant as a butterfly flapping its wings could make the difference between a rainstorm or a hurricane many months later and thousands of miles away. The "initial" in "initial conditions" is any point in time and space you choose. Future generations may find it hard to comprehend the arrogance of the scientific cultural base that was set to be turned around in 1961 when Edward Lorenz took a numeric shortcut that led him to an unexpected new destination.

Chaos was the law of nature; Order was the dream of man.

Henry Adams, American journalist and historian,
1838–1918

Lorenz was tinkering with the simulated weather system he'd been running on his computer, and "rewinding" it back to an earlier point in time. The system generated the weather according to twelve interacting factors such as wind speed, temperature, humidity, and so on. When re-entering one of the factors, he rounded down from 0.506127 to 0.506, assuming that such an insignificant change would make no difference. Its effect on the overall system would be about as significant as the effect of a flapping butterfly's wing upon the wind speed. This calculation made no difference at first, but then the weather system changed slightly and within a few months had developed into a completely unrecognizable weather system. The butterfly didn't actually cause or trigger anything. The discovery was that the actions of every single part of a complex system, however insignificant they may appear, have an effect upon the whole. Edward Lorenz later wished he'd called it the "Seagull Effect" since that bigger wingspan would have made the concept more credible.

If the significance of a mere butterfly's wing flap is hard to swallow, let me give you an easier example. There are many in your own life that you will recall and many more that you will never even recognize. Something as insignificant as a pause to pass wind can make you miss a bus, whereby you meet someone at the bus stop and strike up a conversation—the script can go anywhere from here, but that conversation could change your career, your love life, or simply trigger you to go see a movie that will change in subtle ways your reactions and relationships with the world thereafter. Every input and output, however insignificant, affects not only your life but also the future of the world in some small way, and often quite dramatically in seemingly unrelated ways.

I'm not afraid of chaos and I'm happy talking to strangers. I really love not knowing where I'm going.

Fiona Shaw, Irish actress and director, 1958–

The butterfly of chaos theory has made nonsense of all the linear projections made by politicians, economists, and their ilk. In today's ever more complex world, that which changes history is rarely predicted—the rise of Napoleon; the great stock market crash of 1929; the collapse of the Iron Curtain; AIDS; the Internet; 9/11; the Arab Spring; Occupy. On more mundane matters as well, the forecasts and projections of the "experts" can often be dramatically out of touch with reality, whether we are looking at weather or economic statistics.

What chaos theory proves, which may now seem self-evident to you, is that even if the weather forecasters had one million non-invasive data inputs per cubic millimeter of planet Earth, accurate to a hundred decimal places, they would still not be able to forecast exactly when it might rain in a few weeks, or when an unexpected butterfly may pass by. All they can hope for is that it all goes as it has in previous years, following established trends and averages. There will always be scope for dramatic and unpredicted weather events as well as unforeseen collapses of markets and governments. Sometimes, even when we are able foresee these events, we still walk blindly into them, to the perpetual bewilderment of future generations.

For many years meteorologists have worked on the principle that if we had enough data available we would be able to get the weather forecasts absolutely right. In the late 1950s it was believed that as we increased our knowledge of weather systems and our chemical and technical ability, we would ultimately gain control over the weather of the world. The ingrained principle of determinism that led to such fanciful thinking has now been overturned in the world of science.

The state has, for many years, been firmly run on the equally unsupportable principle that with enough data and sufficient force applied in the right places, it can not only accurately predict the course of society, but actually direct and manipulate it at will. We now are faced with the evidence that it is not possible to achieve this objective through the forcing of some parts of a complex system, and we have centuries of experience of the state's manipulations going wrong. Yet many of us still hang onto the hope that some day they will find a way to successfully shape society to their plans, from the top down, and that those plans will have our best interests at heart. Hang in there if you like.

Is there any reason to suppose that human society, alone in the Universe, is somehow exempt from the rules that everywhere else govern the development of stable yet adaptable complex systems? The answer to this question becomes abundantly more clear by the year.

> *Every time the government attempts to handle our affairs, it costs more and the results are worse than if we had handled them ourselves.*
>
> Benjamin Constant, Swiss writer and politician 1767–1830

We do not get government through the hapless attempts of the state to forcibly control and shape society. Instead we get interference in the development of the self-governing structures that our complex society would otherwise produce. This process is always at our cost and usually to our cost, which is to say *we* pay the bills and *we* suffer the consequences.

Many of these self-governing structures already do exist in our society and flow so smoothly that we do not even recognize them. Like the fractal patterns of the natural world, our own society has an invisible order and pattern to it that is not superimposed from above, but created by a network of freely operating interdependent systems. Many of these self-governing structures have been developed over the course of many generations, changing and adapting to a changing society. Whilst the components of these structures may be subject to some forced interface with the state, the pattern of this system is largely self-organized.

We are not aware, nor have we needed to be, of the invisible structure that combines to feed a large city on a daily basis, nor of the multi-layered systems that permeate our society, ensuring we are clothed, fed, read, entertained, connected, and usually able to find a hot drink at a cafe somewhere not too far from our home. When the state directs things, we call it government, but when we let them happen by themselves with no fuss or mess, we don't call them anything. We are not even aware that there might be a problem when we always have the "solution" to it woven into the fabric of our lives.

Chaos theory now recognizes the patterns that evolve in complex systems and shows us why the severed feedback loop between the state and society (its "clientele") prevents the state from providing viable governance. Instead of governing society, the state seeks to dictate and enforce the conditions that it thinks to be "best" for society in some generally agreed sense, while stripping that society of the means to develop its own real solutions.

For the past few hundred or few thousand years, depending on geography, the top-down coercive state has been telling us that its existence is essential to society (for some indigenous inhabitants of the rainforest this is an even newer concept). We have agreed with this over those years either because of the threat of damage should we not, or because everyone else did and it is comfortable to feel normal. The state seemed to be something we had created because we needed it, despite its often glaring imperfections. History shows us a succession of failed states going back into history, and now science shows us why top-down control does not work, demonstrating that bottom-up self-organization does. Without that scientific insight we could be forgiven for thinking that our latest varia-tion of the state is somehow up to date and evolving. With that insight we realize that the state is not up to date, nor was it ever such. Yes, the state is out of date.

Freedom is just Chaos, with better lighting.

Alan Dean Foster, American author, 1946–

5

Playing God?

When we accuse people of "playing God," it is usually because they have over-ridden the natural flow of events in order to make things run to a plan they had pre-determined. Well, however you wish to define your supreme God character, this doesn't seem to be the way that He, She, or It goes about things.

You could be forgiven for suspecting that some of the breath-taking wonders of the natural world were planned by a divine being. But the Universe and everything in it was evidently not planned by somebody kind of like us but one heck of a lot smarter—God sitting at the Universal Computer, plotting out all those microbes, molecules, and chromosomes; making peaches soft and iron hard; deciding where the mountains and deserts go, and who the lightning strikes. If you were God, wouldn't you have better things to do? Wouldn't you build some handy labor-saving device into the system that made things work out on their own, giving you the time to chill out and enjoy the more important aspects of being universal energy?

However you define divinity, we now inhabit a universe in which everything is free to create its own future. God does not work to a predetermined plan, but the Universe itself creates an order through allowing the energetic forces at play to work with the materials to hand. The science of chaos theory has recognized that when you have a large number of seemingly unconnected events flowing freely, they are more likely to form relationships, a flowing stability, and order than they are to descend into a mess of tangled relationships that don't work. This looks like a bona fide universal rule, yet for a long time humankind has worked on the principle that order must be deterministically shaped from the chaos; order and stability were created according to either our master plan or our linear interpretation of God's divine plan. Today's mainstream God of Christianity, Islam, and Judaism is often perceived to have planned our world in detail, and dictated how we should behave, right down to specifics of hair styles, choice of diet, and types of sex.

Of course, it is the failure of these top-down commandments, God-given or man-made, that is the most frequent cause of grief to our species. For reasons that we all innately understand, our emotional reaction to the death of tens of thousands in a devastating earthquake or tsunami is dwarfed by the horror of deaths inflicted by evil-doing humans when bombs are ripping apart innocent shoppers and commuters—people like us. The fifty million human lives claimed by the great flu of 1918 and 1919 are eclipsed by the eight and a half million slaughtered over the prior four years in World War I. The hundreds of thousands of lives lost in the tsunami of 2006 will have faded into the past long before the memory of the 2,800 lost when the Twin Towers were reduced to dust five years earlier. Hurricanes blow, volcanoes erupt, tectonic plates quake, waters flood, people are lost, and this we have been living with and living through for a few million years. We live on the Earth and must accept that it has a destiny of its own that may or may not fit in with where we choose to locate cities and our personal lifetime goals. But the impersonal and intentional killing by human beings of other human beings makes us shudder at a more visceral level.

Putting our trust in God and loving God form the core of many religious teachings, combined with the overall rule of showing consideration to others. Yet by the time this trust and love are filtered through central control they too often become obedience to the church's instructions and fear of the Lord should you disobey them. The greatest prophets sought to share their wisdom with us so that we might better pursue the path of being fulfilled and happy human beings. These prophets sought to give us principles and tools, not preachers and rules.

God's power is based on allowing every element of creation to be free to create and enjoy its own destiny in a universe that seems magically programmed to create order from the bottom up. We enjoy this order in everything from the delicate skin of our Earth's atmosphere to the complex colony of bacteria that operate within our gut to help us turn what we eat into what we are. This free system works, and when we use our considerable intellectual powers to construct an artificial structure that attempts to forcibly control the system, we are not playing at being God—we are ignoring and obstructing the greatest tool that God built into the Universe.

As human beings, we are endowed with freedom of choice, and we cannot shuffle off our responsibility upon the shoulders of God or nature. We must shoulder it ourselves. It is our responsibility.

Arnold J. Toynbee, British historian, 1889–1975

6

Can You Believe Them?

Wherever you may be on this planet, the political power holders are probably telling you that everything is going to be all right as long as they get to keep holding the controls for long enough. They will be taking credit for anything that is functioning well in society and putting blame elsewhere for whatever is going wrong. For long they have been assuring us that their policies and programs will eventually bring about full employment, a roof over every head, honest and responsible politicians and public servants, improved health, reduced taxation, no terrorists, and less crime on our streets.

Do you believe them? Do you truly believe that the problems facing society will be sorted out when the right person or party gets into power, and that some new rearrangement of the controls will properly "tune" the economic climate and bring about all the benefits promised by that person or party? Or do you, like most people interested in the process, think primarily in terms of which party or person is the lesser evil, sometimes even overriding that simple logic in order to punish those who are currently IN power?

You should think about these questions more deeply than you are accustomed to, since, if you are the average citizen of a "developed" nation, over half of your working life and productivity is devoted to supporting the state. When we total up income tax, corporation tax, import duty, excise tax (gasoline, tobacco, alcohol, and so on), sales tax, property tax, road tax, capital gains tax, death duties, airport tax, plus a myriad of other snips and charges for things once included in our taxes, we find that well over half of our income or earnings is harvested by the state, and we have no choice in the matter. Do you really believe that with all this money the state will one day get it miraculously right, cease being a burden on the back of society, and become a true servant of our society, rather than a Frankenstein-like creation to be milked by politicians, manipulated by special interest groups, lobbied by big business, and courted for supplies by war makers around the world, to mention but a few of its major functions?

Do not believe them. The larger any state becomes, the greater a burden it becomes to society as a whole. It used to be uncommon for both partners in a relationship to need wage-earning jobs, being less of a necessity when overall taxation was less than half of today's level. The evidence has often been that the more money the state spends on any particular problem, the worse it has become over the long term. The more determined its efforts to coercively control crime and disorder, the more holes appear in the moral fabric of society. Cybercrime is the most recent hole in that moral fabric, and one which is often difficult to measure or even detect. For many unfortunate souls, morality has been reduced to not getting caught or sticking to the letter of the law when ripping off their victims. Thus, it is preposterous that a giant seed supplier could sue farmers for letting its migrating pollen have sex with the soybeans in their field. But it is legal, and the suffering of those who lost their family farms and their fortunes figures nowhere in the crime statistics.

Compared to just a century ago, an inconceivable amount of our behavior is now determined by legislation, a process slowly replacing the need for any moral code to arise within the community. I'm not talking about the morality of killing or stealing, but of legislating things like race- and gender-related attitudes to such a degree that we are less able to identify bigoted and prejudiced people in our midst because they are legally restrained from expressing their twisted feelings. We do not require a coercive state to dictate politically correct behavior and put people in jail for their faulty mental attitudes, even if they are deeply offensive to some of us.

> *I am absolutely opposed to political correctness. You cannot confront hate speech until you've experienced it. You need to hear every side of the issue instead of just one.*
>
> Jane Elliott, American anti-racism activist, 1933–

When so much of how we must behave is determined by statute law, we can easily forget the meaning of personal responsibility and risk, confusing morality with sticking to the regulations. We are asked to believe that if they have enough powers and enough of our money to power them and their plans then they can draft legislation to deal with all life's problems. It's not surprising that the majority of our politicians are lawyers who are born and bred around conflict, with resolution achieved by the stick of statute. Now and again they will eliminate a problem peaceably, permanently, and inexpensively, but this is not common. As chaos theory shows us, stringent controls directing specific elements of a system cut into the feedback loops linking the entire system together—links that enable an ongoing and flexible stability to develop.

The modern totalitarian state may come in any color of the political spectrum, as it seeks to establish its vision of perfect order by extending the reach of legislation deeper into our lives. They may get the trains running on time and build good roads but their rigid plans eventually suffer a painful collapse, revolution, or conquest by either a would-be liberator or a new enslaver. In the still-functioning European Union of the 2010s, we are beginning to see the awful downside of many carefully devised economic plans. At the time of this writing, we're not sure whether the plot will lead to collapse, revolution, another downstream kick, or a situation where we discover that we have been sold to the banks. There are no liberators in sight and, quite frankly, who would want to invade? Watch this space.

Uncommon Political Aptitude Test

This "Uncommon Political Aptitude Test" appears on one of the flyers for "Uncommon Sense," the 1998 precursor to this book.

Give them (the UN, EU, Bush, Blair, Putin, Mugabe, and so on) enough time, money, and expertise and they would

A: Eventually get this topsy-turvy world into shape—with full employment, safe food, a stable climate, fading crime, world peace, and no hungry children.

B: Eventually squander it all and take us down the drain with them, using said time, money, and expertise to ensure they are the last bit of frothy scum going down.

If you answered A: You really need this book but probably aren't ready for it yet—good luck.

If you answered B: This book will give you real cause for optimism—and make sense of the madness. Do your head a favor.

7

Natural Government versus State Control

The Internet is the first thing that humanity has built that humanity doesn't understand, the largest experiment in anarchy that we have ever had.

Eric Schmidt, executive chairman of Google, 1955–

Without the state, who would run the emergency services, educate our children, set speed limits, and all the rest? This is the first thought that usually springs to mind. The former rulers of the communist Soviet Union, when taken on a tour of an American supermarket, could not imagine that a nation could feed itself without top-down regulation, and assumed the supermarket to be phony and set up for the sole purpose of impressing them. For nine years after the end of World War II, Britain maintained food rationing because its rulers had become so used to it that they could not believe such a complex and important process would be able to somehow self-organize all on its own. They had a point—it seems that only chaos theory can explain the miracle of how cities the size of London, Bombay, New York, or Mexico City conspire to feed all of the inhabitants according to their own tastes and means on a daily basis without any central organization or planning. It is government from the bottom up, by the people. It is true democracy. Though we rarely recognize or acknowledge the invisible natural government that arises in a free food chain, it keeps our stomachs and larders filled with whatever we desire.

And this miraculous stuff isn't just happening in the food industry. Though some elements of our society have been regulated and run by a state of some sort or another for more than a few centuries, most of that which we rely on is actually largely out of their hands and working very well. We can take many things for granted from our own natural government. Look around, examine your own life, and ask what it is that you enjoy and rely on from the progress of society, and without regard to economic swings. As well as being able to regularly feed yourself, you are probably able to be clothed, furnish your living space, communicate by many means, sell and trade your skills, read literature, make phone calls, travel from place to place, watch TV or video, use a computer, insure against the risks of life, listen to music, party, and do many of the other things we associate with living our lives. But regardless of era or access, none of these products or activities were conceived or initially developed by any state—they, together with almost everything we can depend upon with some reliability, emerged from the chaotic interaction of a society made up of billions of freely acting human beings. The patterns that arise from this chaotic exchange form most of the fabric of our daily lives, and are governed from the bottom up, by the people. It is democracy without the demagogues.

Even a highly complex structure like the international airline industry started off with no more than two bicycle mechanics pursuing a personal dream. The Wright brothers could never in their wildest dreams have envisioned the scale of the industry that was to follow their invention of the flying machine, nor imagine its effect upon our mobility as a civilization. Most of the aviation industry evolved over the past hundred years from the chaos of our changing culture. No government directive created the package holiday, or decreed that by the year 2000 we would be able to fly across the Atlantic and back in under a day for less than a week's earnings, with a vegetarian meal option. It was neither planned nor implemented by a central body using deterministic techniques. As a result, airplane travel became less expensive, safer, and easier to use during its first hundred years. Certainly, the air industry got a booster from the state's wars through free pilot training and cheap surplus airplanes after World War II. They are clawing that back though, with many flights today costing as much in tax as in airline charges. To this must be added the endless delays and inconvenience to travelers now brought about by the inclusion of air transport in the war between the state and its opponents.

If you search through history for contributions to society that had their origins in state planning or state programs, you will find a frugal harvest—things like margarine, radar, and beet sugar. Do not give the state credit for the amazing progress and order that our society has created, often after having to overcome the resistance and regulations and predation of the state.

The state sees most radical changes to the established order as a threat to its existence. Typewriter ownership was carefully controlled in regions of the former Soviet Union because it let people communicate. For decades the BBC ruled the British airwaves and CB radio was banned on arrival in the 1970s. But humanity pushes forward, overcoming state resistance and evolving our culture. And now the genie is out of the bottle—we are connected online. The astonishing ease of sharing information opens our eyes to things we might never have imagined; from the iniquitous to the inspirational. Social media has enabled the dreaded masses to self-assemble into spontaneous leaderless actions, whether in the streets of Egypt and Tunisia or occupying Wall Street, USA. We can now see why authoritarian states were so edgy about letting people communicate with each other.

When the original Internet structure was envisioned as a means of linking computers together and distributing information, few could have imagined how it would blossom and evolve when untold billions of computers and cell phones were meshed together into the appropriately named World Wide Web. Unprecedented in human history, a border-free and unlimited new territory was created on the map of the human race, created through human co-inspiration instead of conspiracy and plot. It is ours, and under attack.

That the Internet has remained free to this day is in large part due to the efforts of those such as the Electronic Freedom Foundation. That organization, spawned in 1990 when the word "Internet" meant nothing to most, has ever since been combating relentless government and corporate attempts to control the Internet. China has managed to impose borders on its peoples' access to cyberspace, and Uncle Sam has been furtively keeping track of everything US citizens do online or with their mobile phones. Fear of terrorists and pedophiles are two of the tools being used in their pursuit of greater control. Fear of any kind usually works.

I have built my organization upon fear.

Al Capone, American gangster, 1899–1947

It is the billions of free will actions by individuals and institutions and businesses throughout the globe that every moment create and shape the Internet, the cyberspace we surf through without thought of national borders, boundaries, and visas, of whether we're in California, Hong Kong, London, or Cape Town. Let us hope that we, those millions of individuals, are resilient and resourceful enough to keep the Internet free and flowing. In overruling an attempt in 1996 by the US government to control the Internet, Judge Stewart Dalzell stated: "Just as the strength of the Internet is Chaos, so the strength of our liberty depends upon the chaos and cacophony of the unfettered speech the First Amendment protects."

We would like to think the state has only our best interests at heart, even though its record on issues of safety and pollution usually lags far behind the public awareness that would otherwise prompt corporate and evolutionary change. For decades we have watched the state stifle or ignore damning evidence on the dangers of asbestos, nuclear accidents, hydrogenated fats, artificial sweeteners, pesticide poisoning, and genetically modified foods. The state is often to be seen harassing, silencing, and even imprisoning those pioneers who seek to raise public awareness of these issues, be they research scientists with unwelcome findings, organizations such as Greenpeace, or individuals who wish to express their protest with a freewheeling DIY lifestyle.

Government legislation actually protecting us from danger, when and if it comes about, usually follows the change that society is already implementing. Even slavery was already out of practice in half of the United States and most of Europe when President Lincoln waged war on his neighbors in the South. The Civil War was not initiated because the South practiced slavery, but because Southerners sought to dissolve the political union that had been agreed upon eighty years earlier. Only after the war commenced did the abolition of slavery became an official cause—to rally moral support and ensure God was on the right side.

If 60 percent of businesses were to rely upon slaves or child laborers to ply their trade, there would be no climate for any state to ban these practices. Even today, revelations about our supply chain's connections to child labor and exploitative practice in Asia come from charities and action groups, not from our national governments. Consumers can stop these practices quite effectively if they wish to, and have prompted such change throughout history, often without even being aware of the process. The reason there are virtually no GMO products on sale in the European food chain is not because they are illegal but because they must be labeled as GMO, and people remain unconvinced on the benefits versus the risks.

Because of the state's often inadequate setting of minimum "safe" levels for various toxins that are placed into our food and environment, we lose the ability to obtain justice from the original creators of these products when they are subsequently found to have damaged our lives. Because Company X kept to the government standards, it does not have to be responsible for the damage its products create. This might, one suspects, lead to less consideration for those long-term consequences when the products are initially introduced, or when the first awareness comes that there may be damaging consequences to their use. In some cases it may lead to intensive lobbying by Company X, persuading the government to overlook negative research about, for instance, a low-calorie sweetener it seeks to introduce, thereby giving the product state approval and the company freedom from liability. The climate is perfect for a widespread "what can we get away with" approach to moral responsibility.

That government is best which governs least, because its people discipline themselves.

Attributed to Thomas Paine, Thomas Jefferson,
and Henry David Thoreau

(Perhaps they thought it needed repeating)

The cost of financing the state's so-called governing service is enormous and difficult to even measure, representing an added cost to almost everything we do in life beyond taking a breath. Be assured that all those things that are supplied to us "free" from the state are costing us far more as a society than if we were responsible for providing them ourselves. The misrepresentation of health services as being free, in particular, breaks the customer and service provider relationship that we should have with our doctors, and risks turning them into a near priesthood to the sick and infirm. Many of these sick, meanwhile, have been disempowered to the degree that they no longer feel responsible for something as basic as their own health. It makes the "service" highly expensive, and creates a controlled market in which drug companies can charge extortionate prices that include the cost of hiring expensive lobbyists to massage the system.

Unfortunately, when we do seek to take responsibility for our own health and choose alternatives to the state-approved systems, the state enacts laws that restrict or prohibit us from healing with anything other than the techniques of the status quo. One is reminded of the Middle Ages when the administration of any unapproved medical treatment (such as herbs or the laying on of hands) was automatically branded witchcraft and punishable by death. Today the state just kills the companies or careers of those involved—all done, of course, in the interests of public health and pharmaceutical industry profits.

> *It is amazing that people who think we cannot afford to pay for doctors, hospitals, and medication somehow think that we can afford to pay for doctors, hospitals, medication, and a government bureaucracy to administer it.*
>
> Thomas Sowell, American economist and philosopher, 1930–

In addition to the multiple layers of taxation, we have the expensive and wasted effort of trying to live under the attack of the state. When things are "normal," we suffer the constant "requirements" of the state that increase our workload, requiring us to keep abreast with proliferating regulation; to maintain detailed tax records if running a business; to supply regular statistics to government; to make submissions for permissions that often prove confrontational; to pay extortionate fines for minor victimless offenses; and so forth. One could fill a book with well-justified bitching and moaning about the pointless excesses of government. As this author was fined and given a criminal record for non-completion of Great Britain's national census, I feel qualified to question how much sensible use the state has made of prior censuses. Just look at the state of the UK.

So many of our interfaces with the state are confrontational rather than cooperative. On the confrontational world stage we also have the costs of rebuilding war-damaged cities and utility infrastructures, maintaining our maimed and wounded, supporting the homeless refugees, raising the orphans, and feeding the victims of famine, which is more often caused by the activities of war than by weather. Yet we continue to accept this as the price we have to pay for government, a "necessary evil," without considering the alternative option of developing even more of the powerful naturally arising patterns that govern so much of our society already, from the bottom up.

Have you ever wondered why it is that politicians throughout the world are always repeating the mantra of the growth economy? Why is it that the economy must grow every year and what is the great crisis we face if it does not? The answer lies in the simple fact that as the cancer of the state becomes ever larger, ever more of our money is required to support it. This would naturally have the effect of reducing our living standards, were we not continually producing more and more, in order to close the gap. With high economic growth we see our living standards increasing, despite the cancer's growth; with low economic growth we may hold steady; with no growth or negative growth our living standards begin to plummet. In a natural economy, a 2 percent drop in GDP would spell a 2 percent drop in living standards—painful but bearable. In a state-run economy, such a drop spells disaster for the economy. We are seeing this happening today, as a once booming Europe slows down and parts of it grind into reverse.

We do not have the freedom or finances to govern ourselves under the constant burden of the state. Without this burden, and with the consequent release of wealth back to society, it is neither naive nor idealistic to expect that those problems we rely upon the state to manage would be greatly reduced. Products and services would become cheaper, and we would have more funds to deal intelligently with our remaining problems. All that talent wasted on tax avoidance schemes and weapons-design could be put to good use. And we would all benefit from a massive boost in positive enterprise and employment as society rose to meet the challenge of providing those services that the state has been mismanaging for decades and in some cases centuries.

We possess the skills that are needed to rise to the challenge. A successful free society thrived for over a century in medieval Europe at Dithmarschen, on land that farmers had reclaimed from the sea. It prospered without coercive control and taxes, without jails, judges, or armies, until forcibly taken over in 1559 by the Duke of Holstein's cavalry. The people of Dithmarschen had repelled a previous attempt in 1500 at the heroic Battle of Hemmingstedt, when a well-organized militia of one thousand peasant farmers repelled The Great Guard, an army of twelve thousand sent to impose their fealty by force. I am proud to possess genes passed down from my maternal ancestors in Dithmarschen.

Freedom also flourished in Florence, one of Europe's great medieval cities, run by so-called peasant communes that were not beholden to any king or duke. Businesses formed guilds designed to maintain standards and fair dealing. In 1340 the city held ninety thousand inhabitants. There were eight thousand children of both sexes in primary schools, with four universities servicing the six hundred in higher education. There were thirty small hospitals with over one thousand beds in total. It worked.

We must never allow ourselves to be trapped by despair, assuming that something is not possible because it may never have been done. A great teacher of mine assisted me over this hurdle when he made two salient points about the Wright Brothers' invention of the airplane—points that could apply to most of the major discoveries that have advanced our civilization.

1. Was it impossible to fly before the Wright brothers invented the airplane?

2. The Wright brothers did not invent flight by fighting falling.

The answer to the first question is of course no—it was possible to fly, but nobody had figured out how. The point that my teacher, Professor Andrew J. Galambos, was making is that freedom is possible, even though it may not have been very apparent in the recent history of our evolution on this planet.

What we can learn from the second point is that we do not successfully build something by attacking its opposite. You may notice that groups and bodies who set out to "fight" something or launch a "war" on it are rarely successful in their aims, though they may spend vast sums of money and receive much publicity in the course of it. We will not succeed by attacking or fighting the state with variations of its own coercive tools. We can succeed by discovering ways to discourage and disempower the state's interference with our own evolution, putting us on track towards sustainable and effective natural government without need of "central control." It can be done and we can do it, as we are naturally good at this and have the tools.

8

Legitimizing Coercion

One of the greatest damages to society arising from the state is the erosion of our own natural repulsion to coercion as an acceptable mode of behavior. The legitimization of coercion at the top, because it is deemed necessary for the good of the people, percolates down throughout a society that looks to leaders "in charge of things" for a value system.

Let's face it—most of us are naturally repelled by coercive behavior, by people threatening to hit us or damage us if we don't do what they want or disagree with what they say. Most of us are programed by our natural culture and instinct to not do things in this way. We prefer to request, purchase, trade, suggest, or argue as our means of interfacing with the rest of society. The ultimate act of coercion is that of killing another person and this, not coincidentally, is one of the most universal natural taboos found in different societies throughout the world.

Harsh military training is needed to overcome our natural resistance to kill others; even after training, most soldiers shoot to miss. In both World War I and II it was estimated that 80 percent or more of soldiers shot into the air above their enemy, or just didn't shoot. Killing does not come naturally to us. One of the great appeals of the military's new drone technology is that killing has been reduced to the level of a video game. So removed are they from the reality of killing that drone operators routinely refer to the deaths of their fellow human beings as "bug splats."

People are not the killers of the world. It is the organized and rigid belief systems of the world that are expert at convincing us their righteous cause is greater than the value of our individual lives, and the lives of those they exhort us to kill on their behalf. The greatest tragedies of human history have been wreaked upon us by kings, priests, politicians, and nation states—not by the odd mass murderer. And it is likely that the majority of those killers who do arise in society received their initial training in a government uniform.

> *The direct use of force is such a poor solution to any problem, it is generally employed only by small children and large nations.*

> David Friedman, economist, physicist, libertarian, 1945–

For the higher purposes of the state, coercion is now deemed acceptable, and all of the state's instructions to us are backed by the threat that damage will be inflicted upon us if we do not comply. Coercion is the fundamental stick of the state. Almost nothing the state does could be done without it. Let us take a quick trip through coercion and consider the consequences of its use in society. To "coerce" is described by *Collins Unabridged English Dictionary* as "to compel or restrain by force or authority without regard to individual wishes or desires." The lion does not coerce the wildebeest into being his dinner—he just kills it and eats it.

How does the state use coercion on us? Using a simple example like a parking fine, let us say that you absolutely refuse to pay this ticket or spend time in the court process trying to prove, say, that the police had blocked you from returning to your car in time due to a security scare. Anyway, no way are you going to pay a hundred dollars, pounds, or whatever to this uncaring and unresponsive state-sanctioned collection agency. Neither will you run and hide, accept losing your freedom and going to jail, nor will you let anyone impound your car or in any way take your money from you. So what does the state do? They will get your money, and they will coerce you into paying it; assuming that you are a relatively sane person, you will abandon your righteous determination and pay them.

Why? Because coercion ultimately means that if you are not willing to pay the fine or go to jail or run away, you can be killed. Shocking, isn't it? Of course the state has bailiffs and ways of seizing your hundred whatevers before it comes to this. But if you really did not want them to collect their fine and either had no assets or had made them inaccessible, then the state would come to put you in prison for non-payment. If you did not go into hiding or sought to successfully resist this, actively defending yourself from being seized or stunned or gassed, then they would by some means eventually overcome and incarcerate you, or you would avoid going to prison on account of being dead. They will never say, "Well played, mate, we acknowledge your determination as righteous and will no longer press you to pay the fine imposed by our courts."

This is a simple example and an extreme case. Only a nutcase would throw away his or her life over such a small thing as a parking fine. But that is what coercion is—in its rawest purest form, coercion is the province of the armed forces, who make no bones about the principle that might is right. When a soldier or a mugger points a gun at you, you do what you are told because the gun is there and not because you voted for him, or because he has better logic, a nice smile, or God on his side.

Violence is the last refuge of the incompetent.

Isaac Asimov, author and biochemist, 1920–1992

Many crimes, such as stolen property, muggings, or use of counterfeit money, involve coercion. Just about any crime with a victim has involved coercion. It seems reasonable that society should be able to use coercion back to capture and punish the criminals, if necessary forcing them physically to cease and desist their activities, maybe even killing them if they have killed. Organized coercion against these criminals by a police force may well be a moral and reasonable approach and may serve well as a deterrent, but that does not mean that there are not better and more effective methods of dealing with crime and its victims—methods that rely less, or not at all, on the use of coercion. Though some of these methods exist today, many more would have evolved had the state not for so long been claiming a virtual monopoly on both defining crime and dealing with it.

Our entire culture is permeated with coercively backed laws and regulations that do not protect anyone from being a victim of an old-fashioned coercive attack. Here the threat of coercion is used to make us drive slowly, mow our lawns, build according to local government wishes, register newborn children, complete census forms, put the "correct" garbage in bins, and many other simple things. Coercion and a disregard for personal liberty are the essence of those tax collection laws that fund the state's existence. Despite all the laws that supposedly protect us from crime, only the tax collecting laws were strong enough to convict the high-profile Al Capone, acknowledged boss of Chicago's Prohibition-era mafia. What does this tell us of the state's priorities?

The hardest thing to understand in the world is the income tax.

Albert Einstein, theoretical physicist, 1879–1955

Even on the level of a small nuclear family or an extended clan, the constant imprint from the state that purports to govern us all is that coercive techniques are all right when special interests, including those of the "common good," are at stake. Some parents may come to regard their families as mini-states, to be run accordingly, with punishments and the use of coercive "training." I am not objecting to or directing how families should raise children, since experimentation is a part of the evolutionary process and parents have near total power over their children in the fundamentally important early stages of their lives. Because the Universe tends to create successful organisms, we have a good basic programming and most of us would naturally shrink from using coercive techniques when infants and children are involved. This is why kids around the world get away with a lot more misbehaving than do adults.

Do not train children to learning by force and harshness, but direct them to it by what amuses their minds, so that you may be better able to discover with accuracy the peculiar bent of the genius of each.

Plato, 428–347 BCE

However, taking their example from the state, too many parents still think it makes sense to use force and the threat of force to beat their children into submission "for their own good." Though we may not be trained psychologists, most of us know the probable results of this approach. Nevertheless, we can take encouragement from the many instances where individuals have been able to overcome, learn, and grow stronger after exposure to some very nasty treatment during their upbringing.

Because coercion—forcing people to do things—is so fundamental a tool in the state's management of society, it becomes easier for the petty, or the highly organized, thief to rationalize his or her actions by comparing them to the morality of the state and recognizing that even greater crimes are being committed by those who are seen to be our leaders. Leaders lead and others follow, including criminals who share similar levels of self-interest to those leaders. When the Mafia demand protection money from a night-club or restaurant, they are doing just what the taxman does, and in some cases may be giving better service for it and demanding less.

When a lawbreaker bribes a policeman, as can and does happen all over the world, they acknowledge that they both operate within the same flawed moral framework. When businessmen bribe politicians or engage expensive lobbyists in order to generate unfair preferential legislation, they are being led into dishonesty by the coercive facilities of the state. Waste, corruption, and inefficiency on many levels continually permeate state and state-related activities with whistle-blowers often ejected from the system—what does this tell us about the mechanism they are using?

Non-violence leads to the highest ethics, which is the goal of all evolution. Until we stop harming all other living beings, we are still savages.

Thomas A. Edison, 1847–1931

Coercion is, simply, the big divide. With it as the basic enforcing mechanism, society's natural moral evolution is warped and distorted. Coercion disregards the feedback loop. The state cannot survive without coercion and we cannot sustainably evolve with it. As bad as big business can sometimes be, it does not use the coercive mechanism *unless* it is using the state as its agent, and unfortunately this is happening more frequently. The basic remit of any business, big or small, is to perceive and deliver products to us that we want. If they spend money seeking to convince us we want that product, then so be it—that money goes into society's pockets too and is ultimately redistributed among us. It pays for much of our newspapers, TV, and radio. If we pay for a product from business and decide we are unsatisfied by it, we are not coerced into buying it again next week and the month after and the year after that until, at election time, we are given the opportunity to choose another supplier for that same product, a product that we may not actually want.

We must recognize that coercion is not a viable mechanism for change. In the long term it always produces negative results. That we think coercion to be a traditional and natural way to run the world is a frightening situation. The ingrained and often gratuitous use of coercion by states around the world has made it easier for individuals to rationalize away their own violent or oppressive behavior and overcome many of the natural strictures that evolution and society would otherwise place upon us. This is why we must not, in our minds, legitimize coercive behavior as acceptable despite the fact that our so-called leaders use it as their stock in trade. Look into history and see where it got them.

An apt and true reply was given to Alexander the Great by a pirate who had been seized. For when that king had asked the man what he meant by keeping hostile possession of the sea, he answered with bold pride. "What thou meanest by seizing the whole earth; but because I do it with a petty ship, I am called a robber, whilst thou who dost it with a great fleet art styled emperor.

St. Augustine, the City of God, 354–430 AD

The end move in politics is always to pick up a gun.

Buckminster Fuller, architect and futurist, 1895–1983

9

The Constant Confrontation

Whoever is in power got there because they fought their way there, whether using ballots or bullets, arguments or artillery. Those holding the reins of power at the top of the pyramid may change from time to time, but the power structure embedded in the bureaucracy of the state remains in place. This includes the military, the civil service, and the bankers controlling our money supply. The structure in which they thrive was originally brought into existence by kicking out a previous power structure or sometimes even an entire race. There are very few instances in history where power has been willingly relinquished without a fight—very few instances of these "public servants" saying "Hey, we're not very good at this and think somebody else ought to have a shot at it." Paranoid doddering old rulers will grip determinedly the reins of power until they are struck down either by disease, coup, or a popular uprising.

It is safe to assert that no government proper ever had a provision in its organic law for its own termination.

Abraham Lincoln, 1809–1865

The most unpopular regimes continue to exert their will upon a populace when all vestiges of satisfaction or support have gone—holding on until the final humiliation of being trapped in their office, bunker, or bedroom—and then being either shot, hung from the nearest height or processed through the courts they once controlled, and exposed to the contempt of a public they once thought to be "their people." Our civilized elections are still bitterly fought, and often determined by the size of the combatants' war chests, and clever strategic moves. The so-called democracy we enjoy today applies little more than a thin veneer over the basic mechanics of the state, and those mechanics have always hinged on the lever of confrontation.

> *Democracy is the art of saying "nice doggie" until you can find a rock.*

> Wynn Catlin (and other credited sources)

The handful of parties claiming to represent our best interests are usually locked in constant confrontation, only sleeping with each other in the interests of defeating a common enemy. Almost everything you read of the politics of the state is the story of a confrontation between two groups, usually bitterly opposed to each other. Should a government of the day "lose" the vote on a bill in the British Parliament, then it is deemed that they are getting weak and unable to manage the country. This state of confrontation is thought to be, and accepted as, the normal way of doing business for the modern democratic state. And even though the state is ostensibly there to "serve" us, the most common experience that many of us have is that of confrontation—whether over building permits, parking tickets, tax demands, or any other confrontation prompted by the state's desire that we all fit neatly into their plan for the fine-tuning of society.

I do not mean to suggest that society should have no plan or order. When groups of people live together and share resources, they have always developed accepted modes of behavior as a social group. The threat of rejection by the community was at one time a greater regulating agent on our behavior than was the fear of being fined or imprisoned. Even in places where there is no law against going to the supermarket in your underwear, there are few who do so.

The police, as a force on the streets, only developed in most parts of the world towards the end of the nineteenth century. The numbers in prison per capita just a few generations ago were a fraction of those incarcerated today, and the main reason for the increase lies in the rapid growth of laws against behavior or activities that have no actual victim (see chapter 17).

As our politicians promise to make us safer with more regulation and control, supported by higher police budgets, would it not be reasonable to expect them to project a need for fewer prisons resulting from the success of their policies? I would be curious to know if history has ever recorded this happening.

Our stimulus to create self-governing techniques is eroded as the state assumes more and more legislative responsibility for our behavior and morals. When the state takes over morality, we lose it. Look at what we have evolved without confrontation but by ourselves—human to human. We have been singing tunes, beating drums, stroking strings, and blowing through tubes since time immemorial, creating a vast variety of musical styles, with Wikipedia's A–Z of them listing eighty-seven different genres under "B" alone. We can choose from classical, electronic, jazz, punk, opera, trance, rock 'n roll, country, rap, brass band, blues, bossa nova, ambient, and a myriad of other musical styles to tickle our ears. We are allowed to purchase or create any, all or none of them—one has not had to supplant the other, even though they may "battle it out" in the marketplace. We can choose from whole wheat bread, white bread, French bread, naturally leavened bread, rye bread, rolls, buns, pancakes, and many other forms of flour and water to have with our meal. Most in Britain and America have chosen the sliced white loaf, for better or worse. In India the same flour and water options are possible, but the overriding choice is chapati, paratha, or puri. In Japan, they make rice balls. We seem to be managing all right, without legislation determining the shape of a bread's loaf, the width of a slice, the curve of a croissant, or the thickness of a chapati.

There is no need in society for one choice or decision to confront and battle it out with all the other options. However, in the affairs of the state this is the basic mechanism at play, one group opposing another in each decision-making process. The state specializes in making decisions of an either/or nature and this is not really surprising when we consider that the vast majority of politicians are lawyers, trained in winning or losing their case after fighting things out.

By contrast, in society we manage successfully with a both/and policy, allowing individual decision making to play the major part in shaping order. When I visited "communist" East Berlin, just before it rejoined the Western half, the results of these different approaches were clearly apparent in the comparative restaurant menus on offer. There was very little to choose from in the East, where all key decisions were made from the top down, while in the West there was great variety. Likewise, the strategically conscious embrace of the both/and philosophy was a key factor behind the success of the user-friendly Apple computer against IBM, with its rigidly linear operating system.

We may have grievances and problems with existing aspects of our culture, whether they relate to racial awareness, attitudes to the disabled, male domination, dangerous drug usage, or corporate irresponsibility. But we cannot successfully deal with these problems by enlisting the support of the state in a confrontational attack on them. We need only look at the success they have had in their fight against crime, poverty, bank fraud, and in the War on Drugs.

As we now understand from chaos theory and the study of complex systems, the systems that are both stable and flexible are those that cooperate with other systems through an intricate and self-organized network. Cooperation, interdependence, freedom, and flexibility are the key elements to any successful and sustainable system, and they are all qualities notably absent in the confrontational activities of today's state.

> *If the present Congress errs in too much talking, how can it be otherwise in a body to which the people send one hundred and fifty lawyers, whose trade it is to question everything, yield nothing, and talk by the hour?*
>
> Thomas Jefferson, American Founding Father, 1743–1826

10

A Terminal Tool Bag

A brief overview of bureaucratic verbosity is provided by this comparative look at a few historic documents:

98 words	Prayer of St. Francis of Assisi
118 words	23rd Psalm
226 words	Gettysburg Address
1137 words	Declaration of Independence, USA
3500 words	Magna Carta
4543 words	American Constitution
16,662 words	(EC) No 2200/96 organizing EU fruit and veg market

Underlying every action taken by the state is a fundamental belief that something as complex as human society can be regulated by applying the appropriate rule and regulation—the belief that determinism is able to control a complex system. It is no surprise to discover that, without the natural feedback loops, most of the basic mechanisms and tools upon which the state relies are fatally flawed in their construction. Here are just a few examples.

Unrestrained Growth Factor

State structures rarely have any mechanism that adjusts their size to the needs of the occasion, and most commonly measure their success by the level of next year's budget increase. So they overgrow if enough money is available.

It would seem to be a natural desire of most forms of organization to grow and prosper. If not enough money is available after society has been taxed to its limit, the state can and often does print more out of thin air to cover budget overrun, thus providing the basic fuel of inflation. Today's euphemism for this is "quantitative easing," though if anybody else were doing it, he or she would go straight to jail for counterfeiting. On top of this, they borrow from others, using future generations as collateral.

Companies classically grow bigger by supplying better products, more products, or increased services to their customers. They have their faults, sometimes misrepresenting goods, selling substandard products, cheating to gain competitive advantage, or spending more on advertising than their product. But if we, the consumer, stop buying a company's inferior or faulty products, then they do stop growing and actually can become smaller—and eventually even cease to exist. It happens.

The state inexorably expands simply by deciding we need its services to "manage" an ever increasing number of society's needs—needs that it perceives with the supposed mandate of the people's vote (more about that later). Most of those areas that the state now "manages" at great cost were not under its control or management less than one century ago. The state spends much of its time just looking for new things to manage and control, continually passing new laws and regulations, with little thought given to removing previous irrelevant and obsolete ones. This growth of assumed responsibility, and the resulting laws and regulations, is often stimulated by corporate lobbyists who will gain from the new controls, and seems to be checked only by the wealth-creating skills of the society on which it feeds. As long as the money is there to support it, the state will feed on this and grow in influence. When the money supply shrinks, then disorder and chaos set in. In extreme cases one state may seek to sustain its growth by forcibly taking over another nation or acquiring its resources, including people.

The government is like a baby's alimentary canal, with a happy appetite at one end and no responsibility at the other.

Ronald Reagan, US President, 1911–2004

Whether state management is running the road works department of a local council, social security, police force, health service, or the Department of Agriculture, it will always seek to advance its own growth and perceived importance and, unless restrained, will steadily and relentlessly expand. In something as simple as a local roads department in the UK it is obvious that at a certain point there are basically sufficient roads in the community and the actual cost of maintaining the existing system is greatly reduced and easily managed. Yet rather than cut the department back, they proceed with constant rebuilding of the existing road system for an alleged future benefit. The reality is a road system constantly clogged by rebuilding works, only a few of which relate to relevant repair of the existing structure.

Some government road works actually detract from the smooth running of a road, such as the regular replacement of speed bumps; superfluous insertion of traffic lights at roundabouts all over Britain; traffic islands that reshape themselves at regular intervals, dangerously narrowing sections of the road; unsightly and confusing painting and repainting of lines, zig zags and grids of red, white, and yellow; channeling of traffic into forced lanes far ahead of intersections, causing some trapped motorists to desperately try and escape at the last minute; implementation of often unnecessary one-way systems; and building of needless mini-roundabouts at otherwise well-functioning crossroads. The list goes on, as new ways are constantly being sought to annually increase departmental budgets—and this is but one example of a local state service gone berserk. I suspect that readers can think of many local examples.

We will not dwell more on Europe's Common Agricultural Policy, an obvious example of unrestrained growth, other than to recognize that the massive level of fraud associated with it actually boosts its growth and creates more employment within the organization. Fraud is not perceived as a cost by the bureaucrats who run it, even though estimates have put it at up to a third of the CAP budget, equal to many tens of billions of pounds per annum. Fraud prevention is not built into the state's tool bag, though it would be unthinkable to us that any of our major food companies could grow and prosper through fraudulent activities such as short-weighing bags of potatoes, diluting milk with water, or adjusting the total on till receipts (when did you last bother to check the supermarket's arithmetic?).

Bureaucracy gives birth to itself and then expects maternity benefits.

Dale Dauten, American columnist and speaker, 1950–

The Disconnected Factor

Unlike the individual, the small company, or the multinational corporation, the state does not need to ask us or even entice us in order to get its hands on our money; neither do we have any specific say in how it is spent. There is no direct relationship between our money and the product we receive from the state—no joined-up feedback loop. Individual customer feedback is not considered and costly "Have Your Say" schemes are often implemented with the results routinely ignored when not in line with government intentions. Thus, when we become unhappy with a service or stop using a product of the state, we must continue to pay for it; it is only if millions of others are in the same position for many years that a message may get through to the deaf supplier.

Every large company has damage limitation plans well rehearsed for any major product problems that could occur. Companies recall products because they acknowledge that they are faulty and may pose a threat to the health of their consumers. Their insurers are also likely to insist. In 1990, when Perrier found benzene contamination in its water, it recalled all stocks, lost market dominance, and later re-emerged into a much larger world market. Perrier did not emphasize the minimal risk to our health or go on about the greater background danger of some legal food additives. Similiarly, in 2011 alone, over ten million vehicles were recalled by car manufacturers due to flaws in production that had only caused occasional problems.

In examples where the state carries responsibility and things go wrong, the instinctive reaction is to cover up and assure us that everything is just fine. Only some thirty years after the 1957 fire at Britain's Windscale nuclear plant did we begin to learn of the true dangers to which that generation was exposed. It was nearly a year after the Fukushima nuclear disaster that the Japanese government revealed it had known of the meltdowns when it was telling us there was no melt-down, and that it had considered evacuating Tokyo. Now they tell us it will take forty years to clean it up. For decades the state assured us that many now banned pesticides, domestic products, and food additives were safe, until campaigners, public opinion, and overwhelming scientific evidence finally forced their hand. Asbestos, known to be toxic since at least 1898, is a case in point. Aspartame and GM foods may well join the club. The state does not take responsibility for hav-ing assured us that toxic products were safe, on the grounds of having listened carefully to the government scientists who said what they were expected to say. Those who speak out, such as Dr. Arpad Pusztai (GM potatoes) and Dr. David Nutt (cannabis), lose their jobs.

Can you recall an occasion when there has been a release of radiation or toxic pollution into the air or water and the government has told us that this is likely to result in XYZ extra birth defects, allergies, and cancers in the decades to come? Instead we see these numbers inexorably rising while we are assured that everything is okay. Governments plan more potentially devastating nuclear power plants while still not having figured out how to "bury" the hundreds of plants now nearing the end of their working lifespan, nor how to protect future generations from two thousand tons of plutonium, which will remain toxic for tens of thousands of years. During the Mad Cow Disease debacle, the British were assured that their beef was still the best in the world; the scare was depicted as silly foreign hysteria that we Brits with our stiff upper lips (and spongy brains) should not worry about. Instead the public was fed stories about the plight of poor farmers and the great British beef industry. Can you ever imagine Heinz telling us it is okay that one in a million of its famous tins of baked beans might trigger a potentially fatal brain disease but we must stick by this great British product?

Repression

One of the most time-honored tools of the state is straightforward repression to silence dissent and disturbance. This often works as a temporary "cure" but has a disturbing tendency to lead to greater unrest and disorder further down the line. It can work permanently, and has done, when extended to the complete extermination of dissenters, but it does often backfire. When the state still controlled all radio channels in the UK, to be "banned by the BBC" was often a sure ticket to success. It certainly didn't hurt sales of "Let's Spend the Night Together," the Rolling Stones hit of 1967 deemed rudely suggestive by the state broadcaster. Repression of a small problem will often stimulate enough interest to make it a big problem or a big success. We see how the suppression of soft drugs has led to an escalating use of more harmful harder drugs. How many once-suppressed "terrorists" are now in charge of entire nations? Strong repression also creates the classic situation where ten new converts to the "cause" may spring up for every one that is knocked down. History is filled with examples, including the Arab Spring and the worldwide Occupy movement that it appeared to trigger. Somehow when the cause is righteous, and even when it is not, the power that is applied as repression can mysteriously transfer itself to those at whom it is directed.

The seed of revolution is repression.

Woodrow Wilson, US President, 1856–1924

Direct Support

We all know that when you raise or lower the price of a can of beans or a pair of boots, this will have the overall effect of either lowering or raising sales of that item. We know that if you offer more pay for a job, there will be more applicants of a generally higher caliber.

However heartless it sounds in today's climate of desperation, it is still undeniable that the more money the state pays us for being in one of the "victim" categories, the more of those "victims" there will be, whether they be the unemployed, single mothers, the rent-challenged, or the disabled. As a wheelchair user myself, I regularly see the clearly able-bodied jumping in and out of cars displaying the official blue disabled badge. I have met many who milk the system for all they can get, regardless of their physical capacity to look after themselves.

Of all tyrannies a tyranny sincerely exercised for the good of its victims may be the most oppressive.

C. S. Lewis, medievalist and theologian, 1898–1963

It may well be implicit in a successful society to charitably help victims of circumstance to overcome hardship and misfortune whether by cash support or other more integral means as they evolve. I maintain that empathy and charity are part of being a whole human being and that the heart and intellect of humanity would be big enough to care for the less fortunate if its pockets were deeper. But the state simply perpetuates the problem by paying out more and more, while having no vested interest in actually changing the situation that provides its bureaucrats with a living. How many examples do we have of government bodies set up to eliminate a problem actually eliminating it, shutting down their operations, and going home?

In many privately funded charity organizations we have been witnessing an evolution towards helping victims climb out of the poverty trap by supplying wells, low-tech farming equipment, education, and increasingly, a market offering a fair price for their products in the West. This is the type of support that changes the situation rather than prolonging it.

Increasingly in the past century, the state has assumed more of the protective, supporting maternal role in society, always seeking to be there with a breast full of the milk of human kindness when we are in trouble; taking care of all those things that we once had to look after for ourselves when we left our parental home to become responsible adults. What the state feeds us is not milk but the polluted remnants of its own plunder from society—that which survives all those inflated salaries, palaces, wars, and harebrained schemes. The money coming back has lost its meaning and its ownership— and is often expended on something other than that which was intended. It is a poisonous breast on which we suck, individuals and business alike, and in the obsession with "getting our share" of the state handout, we both compromise our own integrity and trample on the true rights of others.

Government is the great fiction, through which everybody endeavors to live at the expense of everybody else.

Frédéric Bastiat, French economist, 1801–1850

The state-given right to suck at its sorry breast is one of the basic factors underlying most of the regulations governing our freedom to cross borderlines drawn on the map by the developed nations of the world. And the proffering of this breast stimulates unnatural movements of people, often attracted by the free lunch rather than by opportunity and change. Living without the state will mean putting some trust in the abundant milk of the great Universe of which we are a part. This Universe is far more worthy of that trust than are the pumped up politicians constantly telling us that "Mother knows best and father will punish you if you disagree."

Attack It!

A classic approach by the state to dealing with problems in our society is to set up structures that are designed to relentlessly attack these problems. These structures then become prone to the "Unrestrained Growth" principle discussed earlier, whereby their growth is stimulated by the increase in size or severity of whatever problem they are seeking to address.

Thus, even an honest police force waging a genuine war on crime is subject to the principle that if they are successful they reduce their employment levels and perceived importance. Yet if crime goes up, they achieve increased importance and attract bigger budgets. I give the police the benefit of the doubt and do not suggest that they consciously encourage crime in order to build up their departments. But I must also give the organizing powers of chaos and the market enough credit to realize that this inbuilt principle does not support the successful operation of the system. A clear example of this is the abundance of laws against victimless crimes, such as the drug laws, which build up police numbers fighting an unwinnable war that is diverting much-needed skills and resources from combating those crimes that involve victims.

When drugs are legalized, those forces fighting the War on Drugs will need new crimes to fight, just as happened in the 1990s when the security forces at MI6 transferred a large portion of their budget from the reduced Russian and Irish threats to combating the newly perceived threat to liberty posed by environmentalists, animal rights activists, and anti-road protesters in the UK. The world's military powers were distraught when the Cold War ended, a situation helpfully resolved by invading Iraq and Afghanistan to fight terrorism and gift democracy. Consequently, terrorism is breaking out all over, serving to renew the fear and convince us to accept more shackles to feel safe. It's straight out of George Orwell's seminal book, *1984*, with vague undefined enemies whose allegiances are always shifting. Our constantly cooked-up fear of terrorists has provided the excuse to move the "cameras" inside our homes too, as the state gives itself the right to snoop through our phone calls, emails, and digital trails.

> *The whole aim of practical politics is to keep the populace alarmed (and hence clamorous to be led to safety) by menacing it with an endless series of hobgoblins, all of them imaginary.*
>
> H. L. Mencken, American writer and the "Sage of Baltimore," 1880–1956

There are many other twisted tools in the tool bag and more keep getting added as the lunacy continues. However thoughtfully designed, the basic foundations of the state undermine its own intentions, be they good or bad. Virtually all of the state's tools and mechanisms are backed by coercion—the use of threats and force to generate the specific structure of order it envisions. The use of coercion disrupts the natural feedback loop through which a free system is able to evolve and adapt to changing circumstances.

> *If you want total security, go to prison. There you're fed, clothed, given medical care and so on. The only thing lacking ... is freedom.*
>
> Dwight D. Eisenhower, US President, 1890–1969

11

Our Problems, Our Solutions

The more laws and restrictions there are,
The poorer people become.
The sharper men's weapons,
The more trouble in the land.
The more ingenious and clever men are,
The more strange things happen.
The more rules and regulations,
The more thieves and robbers.

Lao Tzu, Chinese philosopher, 604–531 BCE

Over the past century, our notions of community and social responsibility have gone from being part of being human to being branches of government, defined by legislation instead of governed by humanity. Why should we think it somehow natural and right that the coercive state be the primary agent through which society deals with difficult problems such as health, unemployment, racial bigotry, child abuse, hunger, and homelessness, to name but a few? The state's growing involvement began as a bold experiment in the early twentieth century, prompted by well-intentioned statesmen, groups, and individuals seeking to ensure a greater level of social care by instituting it as government policy cemented by legislation.

This move towards centralized social management had its seeds in the erosion of human dignity and social well-being arising from the industrial revolution of the nineteenth century. These issues had already led to the establishment of many institutions and foundations, founded by wealthy industrialists with bags of money, or concerned individuals with bags of time. They had no interest in living off the situation, simply in reducing or alleviating it. Most of those bags of money will have by now been either plundered or moved to the safety of offshore tax havens. And for those fortunate enough to have work today, it is often full-time work just keeping up with life, while supporting the insatiable demands of a state seeking to satisfy the insatiable demands made upon it.

We have no basis for assuming that, if the state had not taken control, the very real social problems of the nineteenth century would have remained static and unresolved, any more than we could assume that we would still be bigoted racists and homophobic had these attitudes not been banned by the government. Not long ago, homosexuality was banned by the government. The works of Charles Dickens and their impact upon millions of readers may have been more responsible for changing the social attitudes and practices of nineteenth century England than was any subsequent growth in the law and its enforcers. See how we far we have evolved during the past century without government directives, whether in methods of transportation, information technology, or the rediscovery of our connection to the planet that hosts us. We cannot know how successfully society would have responded to its social problems had it retained responsibility for them, and the funds to support that responsibility. We do know that throughout that century the state, putting its "terminal tool bag" to use, has spawned countless agencies to deal with our problems, institutionalizing many of them in the process. The state thrives on problems.

Much of our decision making, consideration, and life-planning is now bound by the assumption that the state should provide a safety net protecting us from ourselves, instead of just protecting us from another version of themselves on the other side of a borderline. For many thousands of years the state was not charged with looking after many of our problems. In most parts of the world, while there were problems, the overall levels of homelessness, unemployment, burglary, mugging, broken families, murder, suicide, and date rape were lower. They have been increasing since

In recent years, we have seen burglary and some crimes of violence reducing in parts of the world. This has been off-set by a massive increase of identity theft and cybercrime, unknown concepts in the past, which are often undetected and, like banking fraud, rarely included in the crime figures. Rates of death-by-police and suicide and are not included in crime figures, even though suicide is against the law in most parts of the world.

The state has no God-given responsibility to look after us all, whatever may befall us. It is neither a law of nature nor a practice used by any other species on this planet. Once we accept the flawed idea that being cared for by an all-powerful state is the natural order of things, we accept a severe restriction of our freedom. We end up with a hugely expensive structure that is supposed to stop people from sleeping on the streets, being mugged, being unemployed, eating harmful foods, or taking dangerous drugs, while itself exacerbating, if not causing, many of these problems. However, much of that which the state is supposed to prevent continues to thrive, and this should give us pause for thought. The fact that over 70 percent of company bankruptcies and consequent job losses are triggered by unpaid tax demands could give us further cause to pause.

One could be forgiven for suspecting that the more money that is taken from society to spend on a problem, the greater that problem becomes. Statistical evidence all too often supports this suspicion. Big Brother does not deliver value, and the sooner we respond to this realization, the sooner will our problems begin to retreat.

Serious Crime figures (England and Wales) *Source: Ministry of Justice*

YEAR	NOTIFIABLE OFFENSES
1999/00	1,277,900
2000/01	1,264,200
2001/02	1,271,900
2002/03	1,313,100
2003/04	1,330,400
2004/05	1,353,400
2005/06	1,429,800
2006/07	1,482,200

"Notifiable offenses" are those for which records must be kept, ranging from murder to shoplifting.

Cybercrime is not a notifiable offense, even though it is the field of choice for a new generation of online criminals. Why break windows and wield weapons when you can sit at a keyboard? So if somebody steals your life's savings by pretending to be an online bank, it's not worth recording. But if the same person shows you a knife and empties your pockets, then the crime goes on record. No wonder cybercrime is booming.

These gradual increases in notifiable crime took place against a backdrop of proliferating CCTV cameras and improved technology and surveillance techniques, plus a steady increase in both the cost and number of police.

Society, with no duty imposed upon it to look after its poor, problematic, and disaster-struck, still makes a considerable, and effective, effort through charities and institutions formed to deal with those difficult situations. The fact that this contribution from society continues to be substantial, despite the awful ravages of taxation, forces one to consider the resources that society might willingly spend on its problems in a state of peace, freedom, and retained wealth. How many fewer problems would we even have in such a condition?

Institutions exist to look after a vast array of problems, and people become active even to the point of breaking the state's law in their efforts to rectify society's ailments. We find non-governmental groups and organizations forming to support lifeboat services, local fire stations, war orphans, abused horses, threatened woodlands, vital medical research, alcoholics, the severely disabled, and a myriad other areas where a member or members of society have perceived a problem and sought to forge a solution to it, starting only with the chaotic mix of their initial position. The people trying hardest, and having most success at dealing with some of the problems facing our world, are not the governments of the day but organizations started by people who saw a problem and did something about it, rather than expecting somebody else to take responsibility. Greenpeace, the Soil Association, and Friends of the Earth are good examples, as are Amnesty and Human Rights Watch, Alcoholics Anonymous, Boy Scouts, and the Salvation Army.

It's always the small people who change things. It's never the politicians or the big guys. I mean, who pulled down the Berlin wall? It was all the people in the streets. The specialists didn't have a clue the day before.

Luc Besson, French film director, 1959–

On the global level, international aid all too often sees the wealth we created being diverted to the Swiss bank accounts of despots or those profiting from its expenditure on dam projects, power plants, agro-chemicals, and military hardware. The story goes on as every week, throughout the world, there are fresh revelations about current and past wastage, embezzlements, and scandals involving official aid budgets disappearing into black holes and unfinished projects. It happens so often that it is all considered quite normal.

The state has co-opted the duty of care from us in just a few generations, both locally and globally. Yes, of course we need to deal with problems like homelessness, bigotry, poverty, drug dependency, pollution, malnutrition, sexual abuse, poor education, and bad health. But by letting the state assume responsibility for these problems, we often condemn them to becoming worse, as we deprive ourselves (society) of the funds and the motivation that would enable us to be more effective in finding positive and flexible solutions. In some of these cases there would be no problem were society not being stripped of its wealth in the first place.

Everything considered, it is heartening to see just how much time and money we can still assemble for social and ecological causes that will enrich "only" the future of life on planet Earth, not the balance in somebody's bank account. We are human beings, and this is what we do naturally.

12

Voting

It is not good to have a rule of many.

Homer, 800–701 BCE

In matters of conscience, the law of the majority has no place.

Mahatma Gandhi, 1869–1948

The majority never has right on its side. Never I say! That is one of the social lies that a free, thinking man is bound to rebel against. Who makes up the majority in any given country? Is it the wise men or the fools? I think we must agree that the fools are in a terrible overwhelming majority all the wide world over.

Henrik Ibsen, Norwegian playwright, 1828–1906

Revolutions throughout the world have been fought for the right to vote—the magic key that is supposed to put the people in charge. We mark as a great milestone in history the successful battle of the suffragettes for the woman's vote, and the extension of voting rights to those of color in parts of the world. Much is made of the power of the vote as an instrument that gives us a fair and democratic say in how our society and government are run. It is also true that Adolf Hitler and many despotic rulers were the most democratically popular when they assumed power.

The vote does not give us a respite from the yoke of the state—it only provides a means to occasionally change the color of the packaging and to do some tinkering with how the meager amount of money that is sprinkled back gets distributed. Voting is an ingenious and well-meant attempt to translate the wishes of the people into the actions of those who govern them. In practice, however, this rarely happens, and the voting system has led to neither freedom nor true democracy wherever it is used in the world.

> *Perhaps the fact that we have seen millions voting themselves into complete dependence on a tyrant has made our generation understand that to choose one's government is not necessarily to secure freedom.*
>
> Friedrich August von Hayek, Austrian economist and philosopher, 1899–1992

In the first place your vote does not give you, personally, any say whatsoever. It gives the majority a say, and the majority may not have any idea of your own interests and situation. The premise that the majority is somehow "right" about a particular issue, or that there should even be issues that have to be decided in such a mechanical way, is essentially flawed. However, if we take it on board, we realize that the majority will often constitute less than one in five (20 percent) of the population. This is the sum you will end up with after deducting those not eligible to vote for reasons of age or nationality, those who choose not to vote at all, and those who voted for the losing parties. In some countries, such as Australia, the general apathy with the voting process reached such proportions that the state legislated mandatory voting—you must exercise your freedom to choose who rules you or risk going to jail. Presumably this law was passed with the sanction of the few remaining Australian voters at the time the legislation was introduced.

Whether voting by choice or forced to vote, many of those doing so will not be actually voting *for* a specific candidate or party. They will be voting *against* the other side, seeing their vote as supporting the lesser of two or more evils. Sometimes they just want to punish and eject those in power, regardless of who fills the vacuum. Others will cast their votes for purely single-minded reasons—for promised financial support of single mothers, or increases to the military budget—oblivious to the full range of policies.

It makes no difference who you vote for—the two parties are really one party representing 4 percent of the people.

Gore Vidal, American writer, 1925–2012

In our real world voting with the pocketbook, we drink Guinness because we prefer it, not to penalize the other brewers or put them out of business. And if enough of us become disenchanted with a product, then the company producing it has either to diversify successfully or die. With the electoral vote we don't get to stop buying the product, nor do we get to buy a new product; we simply get to change the manufacturer of the product and do so on the basis of sweeping promises that it is under no actual liability to fulfill, and that in practice it seldom does. Whether this promise is to increase employment, reduce taxes, or close inhuman prison camps, the public soon forgets.

Consider for a moment to what extent the body of the state remains constant: its volumes of regulation and law with its uniformed enforcers and legal interpreters; the military and defense establishment; total taxation (relentless in its rise); and the countless departments and offices filled with the vast armies of bureaucrats who run this sorry ship. Are we really to believe that even a major re-sculpture of the tip of the iceberg will make a difference to the passengers on this Titanic?

Some have suggested electronic voting, linked through the Internet, as the new path to better democracy—eliminating all those politicians we love to hate. Though well-meaning, this view fails to recognize that the majority can be and frequently are manipulated by special interests. And of course, it is not unknown for the majority to be wrong about things, all on their own. Frighteningly restrictive laws could be propositioned and passed during moments of public hysteria, or following a gross public deception, or arising from massive misunderstandings. The concept is a serious tweaking of the knobs and controls of the state, but not a way forward. A majority of atheists could pass legislation that bans the practice of organized religions, and if the majority is religious, it might mandate the wearing of headscarves and ban alcohol. Those who wish to control and direct the state's coercive power will soon find ways to influence the voters' minds, however their votes are being expressed and calculated.

Vote for the man who promises least; he'll be the least disappointing.

Bernard Baruch, American financier and statesman, 1870–1965

Voting does not lead us to positive evolutionary change any more than do armed revolutions, insurrections, invasions, or fundamentalist takeovers. It is simply another mechanism for determining who holds the coercive reins of power. The democratic voting system is freedom designed by a committee, a committee of those in power. True freedom is far simpler and a lot more free-flowing.

As the anonymous wall graffiti reads: "Don't vote—it only encourages them." What would happen if we were somehow able to vote against the state itself? You will find a suggestion on this in a later chapter.

> *Voting is simply a way of determining which side is the stronger without putting it to the test of fighting.*

> Henry Louis Mencken, American journalist, 1880–1956

A spoof public newspaper produced by Reclaim the Streets in 1997 and confiscated by the police.

13

Divide and Rule

When you blame others, you give up your power to change.

Dr. Robert Anthony, author

One of the silver linings for the state provided by the new multi-party system of government is that the rulers of the day (the "In Party") are usually able to blame many of the problems facing us upon the last party that was in power (the "Out Party"). Failing this, they assure us that the problem would be much worse if the Out Party were dealing with it. "Let us continue doing a bad job because the Out Party would do an even worse one." After a decade or two of continuous rule, kings, emperors, and dynasties could no longer blame their predecessor, as they had no Out Party.

The flip side of this silver lining works for the Out Party because they can always point at the In Party and declare, with some justification, that most of our problems are being aggravated by what the In Party is doing. The conclusion we are expected to make is that because the Out Party can perceive the connection between the In Party and the problem, they will be able to fix it if we make them the In Party. The strong supporting evidence is that before the In Party took power (when the Out Party was running things), the problem was not as bad as it is today. That evidence, unfortunately, is all too often to hand.

> *The two-party system is like magic black and white squares which look like a staircase at one moment and a checkerboard the next.*
>
> I.F. Stone, American journalist, 1907–1989

You probably had to read that last paragraph closely to avoid being confused by the terms In Party and Out Party. It is hard to follow the thread for the reason that there is so little difference between the two. H.L. Mencken summed it up well when he wrote in 1956: "Under democracy, one party always devotes its chief energies to trying to prove that the other party is unfit to rule—and both commonly succeed, and are right." But it is a handy mechanism for the state and helps to keep us divided in our support of one team or another.

One of the unfortunate side effects of the new multi-party system of deciding who runs the state is that society has been fractured and turned against itself. This occurs as one group of statesmen or would-be statesmen realize they can gain power and support by blaming our problems upon a specific segment of our society, such as the rich, the poor, whites, blacks, Jews, terrorists, child molesters, the economy, drug users, gays, men, non-nuclear families, the non-faithful to some religion, or whatever is convenient. Their approach to dealing with whatever they perceive as a problem is always couched in the language of confrontation. They will attack the problem, ban it, smash it, declare war on it, squeeze it till the pips squeak, pass laws to seize its assets, or force it to conform to the norm.

These statesmen encourage some parts of our naturally changing society to view other parts as a threat. They encourage confrontation among us because this brings them greater power and more problems that need to be controlled. Our mind strays from the ball and we fail to recognize just what it is that is actually retarding society's ability to grow and achieve a more harmonious and stable future. Once convinced that our problems are caused by some errant defect in society, we are easily convinced that only the power of the central state can put things right, through applying force in the right places. This process will typically require extra powers for them and less freedom for us.

A classic tactic, originally credited to Julius Caesar and raised to an art by the British during the days of Empire, was to conquer the enemy through expanding and exploiting existing divisions or creating new ones in a previously harmonious situation. Where existing hostile divisions existed, the alliance of British forces with an already strong ruler would usually guarantee the dominance of that ruler over an expanded territory, and a strong British influence over that ruler.

In order to flip a harmonious situation into a hostile one, the essence is to find out what local differences exist in races, tribes, or religions, and then decide upon an effective way of turning one or more of these groups against the others. There are various techniques, such as fanning the flames of an existing grievance, or staging a "false flag" bombing or assassination that frames the other race or sect. One of the aggrieved groups is then likely to welcome military assistance to help them get even, and with a nip and a tuck, both sides are soon being run by a new protective guardian who is there to protect them from each other. Sound familiar? Prior to the recent politicization of the Middle East by Western powers, Muslim, Christian, and Jew had lived together in relative harmony for many post-Crusades centuries.

It is perhaps not difficult to see that "divide and rule" works as a handy built-in mechanism to maintain our support of the multi-party system. By convincing some of us that some others of us are a threat to their lifestyle, the state enjoins our support to protect us from each other. We easily reach a situation where each one of us thinks that some particular group or activity is responsible for most of society's and our own problems. At least the old kings and emperors only offered to protect us from others of their kind over the hill and had no need to continually manufacture enemies within society to maintain our fealty.

14

Birthright Denied

I was born on the prairies where the wind blew free and there was nothing to break the light of the sun. I was born where there were no enclosures.

Geronimo, Apache chief, 1829–1909

If there is one basic right to which every human being is entitled, it must be the right to *live off the land* on the fruits of the Earth. This is the right enjoyed by every other one of nature's less civilized creations. We have volumes of laws concerning our rights and entitlements covering areas of housing, education, employment, relationships, and discrimination by sex, race, and so forth. Yet how can this mountain of rights be of any value when the most fundamental building block of rights—the right to live in a natural state on the planet Earth—is not only absent but virtually a crime in most developed nations? Every other organism on Earth, whether worm or redwood tree, assumes that it will live off the land with no other support structures or rights embedded in writing.

Though we have come a long way in our evolution, we recognize that until we developed tools and learned to manage fire, we basically lived off the land, and did so for a good while thereafter too. We cherish stories of those who have been cut off from civilization and manage to survive in the wilderness with nothing but nature to provide. Many of us wring our hands with genuine grief when we hear of primitive tribes in Africa or South America being forcibly civilized, or wiped out by disease and avarice.

We are right to be proud of the major achievements we have made in creating tools and structures to advance our civilization and remove us from the rawness of living on the edge of survival. We can keep ourselves warm in hostile climates, travel great distances with relative ease, and communicate with each other across the world at low cost to our pocket or the environment. We live in houses that have evolved a very long way from makeshift tents, caves, or coverings of branches. I like the ease of my lighting and cooking facilities.

In taking these developments of our civilization, however, and instituting them as the natural order of life, and then effectively legislating any other lifestyle out of existence, we are threatening the very ability of our civilization to survive. Survival in this world requires evolution, change, and experimentation with the established order and "way." We have always accepted that parents will look askance at their own children's lifestyle experiments, and wonder what will become of the younger generation. This has been going on for many generations.

Today's environmental experimenters are, consciously or subconsciously, looking at ways to live that are neither dependent on the state, nor threatening and disrespectful to the Earth that supports us. They often need to study volumes of law and legal codes and do unnecessary work in order to reduce the risk of harassment, fines, and even imprisonment. In our development of civilization we have so surrounded ourselves with the often wonderful inventions of our species that it is quite possible to forget that the natural state of our ancestors, not that long ago, did not involve houses and apartments, cars, phones, suitcases, personal documents, lawyers, stereos, policemen, television, travel, couture, and all the other trappings of our life that we sometimes mistake for life itself.

What men value in this world is not rights, but privileges.

Henry Louis Mencken, American journalist, 1880–1956

I do not suggest that the trappings of society are all evil or that we should seek to forgo them for some higher purpose. I do suggest, however, that our society is in mortal danger when it has created a climate in which to live without its trappings is considered and indeed made criminal behavior. Such is the case in England, the United States, and most of the developed world today. In many places, including England, you are not even allowed to pursue this simple lifestyle on land in the countryside that you have purchased. Apparently the state and therefore the fabric of society are threatened if you decide to live self sufficiently in a teepee without electricity, growing your own food, rather than being a "productive" taxpaying member of society. We are *not allowed* to opt out of the so-called benefits of the state, or even to choose just those that we support and believe to be good value for our taxes. Because the state has mandated our entitlement, it is deemed logical and necessary that we should *have to make* our contribution to these benefits—as a ludicrous precondition to being alive on a given part of the planet.

Do not fear to be eccentric, for every opinion now accepted was once eccentric.

Bertrand Russell, British philosopher, 1872–1970

This state-mandated entitlement to the benefits it offers constitutes one of the major rationales used to support the removal of our basic right as humans to move freely on our planet and to cross the borderlines defining who owns which tax collection base. The logical rationale behind this is that we cannot let foreign nationals come into our country and claim a right to "benefits" we have paid for, when they are unemployed, homeless, sick, or otherwise in need. That money is supposed to come back to us, after the bureaucrats' salaries and expenses, maintenance of the military machine, foreign aid projects, and so forth. The reality is that large numbers of non-contributors to the tax pot are benefiting from it, whether foreign nationals or not, whether people or corporations, whether in need or not.

The issue of land rights, and the use of land, is a complex one. Many have recognized that it is impossible to personally possess and be the owner of something as indefinable as a piece of land. A plot of land is a section of Earth that is integrally connected to the rest of the planet through feedback interchanges. It shares air and water with adjoining land, as well as underground communities teeming with life. Its limits extend down into the core of the Earth and upwards to some undefined level approaching our planet's outer atmosphere. Though no one claims to own the air blowing in the wind, nor the oceans' shifting waters, many would agree that we have a common right to their usage and a sacred duty to keep these vital treasures clean.

But however we define a piece of land, we have developed entitlements and rights that we call ownership because the tenancy seems permanent. Custodianship of land and property is part of our culture and arises in many different ways, originally from the raw effort of transforming what was once "raw" land into a farm, a house and garden, or indeed a whole community. This process happens in nature when an oak grove makes its own environment, a city of termites changes the topography of their Earth, or a pride of lions define their hunting area. Property rights are not an alien concept, but we need more understanding and clarity on their basis, and on the need to maintain or make use of that property or place. Perhaps, in the same way that we have discovered new and beneficial cures for humanity through investigating some of the medicines of "primitive" tribes, we could also gain some knowledge and useful tools from investigating their different perceptions of property rights.

Whatever rights over land and land use are indeed necessary and proper for our culture to work successfully, there can be no rationale in a sane society to deny an individual the God-given right to live off the land and to move about on it from time to time, in direct interface with our Earth. The situation becomes ridiculous when we supposedly have a "right" to a home, yet those who choose to temporarily live in a teepee, tree house, or bender on so-called common land, in a roadside lay-by, or on derelict land are forcibly evicted, fined, and threatened with prison. In the state's doomed efforts to guarantee us all decent and proper housing, they have legislated out of existence any viable options between "approved" housing and a cardboard box on the street. This is the very real void in our housing stock. Simple shelters and modest dwellings are neither difficult nor expensive to put together— they are just illegal. There are many supposedly poor countries without housing regulations in which it is unusual to find anyone sleeping permanently on the streets, let alone those who have intelligence and education.

There is no simple solution to how the state excludes from its "benefits" those who would choose not to contribute to its upkeep—those who embrace DIY culture and feel safer entrusting their health and well-being to their own efforts, rather than to the questionable abilities of the modern state. But it is patently obvious that a dangerous hypocrisy exists in a society that outwardly extols the virtues of preserving tribes in the rainforest yet allows its own citizens to be jailed for emulating such a lifestyle in their own land.

> *Our contest is not only whether we ourselves shall be free, but whether there shall be left to mankind an asylum on earth for civil and religious liberty.*
>
> Samuel Adams, American Founding Father, 1722–1803

15

The Thin Borderline

Borders are scratched across the hearts of men
By strangers with a calm, judicial pen,
And when the borders bleed we watch with dread
The lines of ink along the map turn red

Marya Mannes, *Gaza Strip*, 1959

We human beings are one of the few creatures on this planet that may not use their own free will to move from place to place, completely oblivious to borderlines drawn upon the maps of the world. We, the most intelligent and developed species on Earth, have our movement carefully controlled and monitored by states around the world every time we seek to move across a borderline on the map. It was not this way at the turn of the previous century and up until the First World War.

One thing is certain—we will never know peace, stability, or harmony in today's world so long as our lives are ruled by imaginary lines drawn by nation states upon the face of planet Earth. The world has always experienced movements of people over time, whether it was the ancient Gauls' movement from Asia to Northern Europe or today's emigration of

Latin Americans to northern America. In today's increasingly global world we can be riding in a Japanese car powered by Iraqi gasoline to an Indian restaurant cooking on Russian gas, watching Brazilians play football on an iPad manufactured in China. Where are the borders? We are more aware than ever that we are all human beings together upon the same planet, sharing its precious resources. Television, travel, and the border-free world of the World Wide Web have all contributed to the dissolution of borderlines in our minds.

> *While the state exists there is no freedom, when there is freedom there will be no state.*
>
> Vladimir Lenin, 1870–1924, *The State and Revolution*

The drawing of borderlines on maps seeks to define territories over which a specific state has dominion, whether the boundaries were established by geography, at the point of a sword, or across a negotiating table. In whose interest is it to know exactly where that line lies? If you feel a part of German culture and live in Alsace-Lorraine, then you may prefer your bread to be dark and wholegrain. If you feel French, then your preference is likely to be the long white baguette—that much we know. But why should the blood of countless thousands have gone to decide whether your piece of land lies in France or Germany? It matters only to those who claim dominion over us. First and foremost boundaries define the area from which states can demand a slice of our productivity and claim rights to natural resources. That this tax base may also represent some loose or coherent grouping of peoples into a similar culture base is often the case, but not particularly relevant. That cultural base, as discussed elsewhere herein, was not created by government but built by the people, from the bottom up.

Globalism began as a vision of a world with free trade, shared prosperity, and open borders. These are good, even noble things to aim for.

Deepak Chopra, author, healer, and guru, 1947–

Ironically, the notion of nationalism is a sad manifestation of society's acceptance that somebody has got to own us, take our money from us, and lay down the rules without us having much say in the matter at all. It has nothing to do with love of our country and pride in our culture, or anything that is genetically peculiar to human beings. The dedicated follower of nationalism wants people from his or her own nationality to make the rules, rather than be told what to do by foreigners. For the sake of a simple argument, let us suppose that Japan makes better cars than most, China makes better fireworks, France makes better bicycles, America makes better junk food, and England makes better music. So what, you ask? It might equally be argued that Switzerland makes better government, but the government isn't something you can choose—it is imposed on you by the chance of which side of a borderline you were born behind.

The state would have it that nationality is something which the government bestows upon us with an official document testifying to that which is already the case. If you are proud to be American or British, then be so, but do not mix it up with the need to be officially approved by, or connected to, that mixed crowd of lawyers in Washington and Westminster who claim to be guardians of all things American or British while they systematically drain and debilitate the society they feed upon—all those within their strongly defended borderline.

Prior to the First World War and the subsequent leap in the size of Western states, life was very different for the average citizen of these countries. With some exceptions, and not during times of war, citizens were generally free to travel throughout much of the world without visas, time limitations, or excessive contact with bureaucracies. It was a world in which humans could make home virtually anywhere, and move their money and goods from place to place with minimal interference by customs and official controls. Taxation was usually less than 10 percent of national income, sometimes rising above during wars and dropping back below for most of the rest of the time. The price of bread and beer varied little from one century to another.

Of course, when personal travel was less common and less restricted, it was necessary for travelers or immigrants to support themselves wherever they chose to rest their feet. There was no question of them ever receiving support from the state running the area in which they settled. Relatives may have provided housing, medical services, food, money, and so forth to immigrant family members until they were able to become useful members of the community. Today, if you have traveled from country to country or around the globe, you may have suspected that all the form filling and officialdom is actually doing very little other than giving bureaucrats a raison d'etre.

In the world of the credit card, high technology, and instant communications around the globe, we have the ability to positively establish identity and home base whenever circumstances require it, using a standardized document if convenient. This may be required by the airline taking us from A to B but not by the bus company or competing airline doing the same. Our credit and debit cards go a long way toward fulfilling this function already, and pay for goods and services. But such a document or device should not be a prerequisite for existence within a boundary itself, nor for travel outside of it to other parts of this planet. The worldwide communications revolution is rapidly breaking down any cultural barriers between the peoples of Earth. It is time also to wither away the unnatural boundaries erected by the red tape of bureaucracy.

Nationalism is an infantile sickness—it is the measles of the human race.

Albert Einstein, theoretical physicist, 1879–1955

16

Who Owns You?

Find out just what any people will quietly submit to and you have the exact measure of the injustice and wrong which will be imposed upon them.

Frederick Douglass, orator and ex-slave, 1817–1895

You might be under the impression that your life is largely your own, to do with as you please, so long as you do not thereby immorally infringe upon other people's lives. Of course this is how we would all wish it to be, and some might be so complacent as to think that it actually is that way. Yet history continually shows us the degree to which the state regards as its own property the lives of those living within the borderline defining its territory. It would seem apparent that one of the unspoken rules of our world community of nations is that any individual state can do whatever it likes to its own citizens without interference from any other state. Where strategic assets are involved, of course, the moral indignation will sometimes overcome this principle.

This prevalent attitude can and sometimes does lead to acts of genocide—the brutal, systematic murder of millions within the state's own boundaries. We saw this happen to the

Armenians, systematically slaughtered by the Turkish Ottomans from 1915–1916, in a holocaust seldom acknowledged by anyone other than Armenian survivors and their descendants. Nobody outside of Germany was very concerned about Hitler's mass murder of German Jews and gypsies, until Hitler extended across his own borders and started killing foreign nationals. Pol Pot systematically murdered millions of his fellow Cambodians while the world looked on. Millions of Russian peasants were starved to death by Stalin, and the world was not concerned. The unwarranted murders continue today, whether in the Middle East, East Timor, the Amazon, Tiananmen Square, Waco, or Nigeria—just read the Amnesty International literature if you need more red spots on the world map. In America today, we find more individuals in jail for drug offenses, primarily nonviolent, than there are prisoners in the rest of the world put together. And the world is not concerned.

There is rare condemnation of these activities and even rarer action to stop them. Indeed, it is more likely that the developed and civilized nations of the world will be falling over themselves to supply the deadly tools of oppression to the states perpetrating these genocidal activities; tools such as attack helicopters and jets, crowd control technology, Taser guns, electric prods, incarceration equipment, and a full menu of gas from CS to old-fashioned tear gas. Only when these supplying nations can clearly see that their old allies' days are over will they switch sides and align themselves with the aspirations of their anticipated new customers.

One of the rare exceptions to world indifference was the peculiar case of South Africa, where legalized suppression of black people provoked ongoing world outrage. This took the form of sporting boycotts and support of the blacks fighting apartheid—action which probably led to an earlier demise of the onerous apartheid rule than would otherwise have happened. However, had the government of South Africa been run by blacks subjugating blacks of another tribe, there would have been little outrage, and their leaders would still be discussing their nation's affairs with other world leaders.

> *There are sixteen million oppressed blacks in South Africa. But some four hundred million people live elsewhere in black Africa, a majority under despotic rule. Why is so little attention given to their plight?*
>
> George Ayittey, Ghanaian economist and author, 1945–

Every country in the world views you as the absolute property of the state running the country of which you are a national, even though your own state will often try to persuade you that your statesmen are "public servants" and you are a free person. We never hear of Malaysia's draconian drug sentences when Malaysians are being executed or of Saudi Arabians who are tortured, imprisoned, or executed for their beliefs. But when an American teenager or a British grandmother is threatened with execution overseas, the world comes to attention. Few seem to care much when a foreign regime is violently opressing its own citizens, unless race issues are involved. When different countries or would-be countries start shooting at each other, the United Nations may step in, set up some UN safe zones, and hope for the best.

In today's new world order we are finding special "humanitarian" exceptions to this longstanding "do what you like on your own turf" rule. When there are significant mineral or strategic assets in the country being abused by a despot, some states become more willing to intervene on the suffering people's behalf. Rebel forces, relentless in their pursuit of the privileges of power, easily pledge away their nations' precious assets to get the job done; they're easy to part with when you don't own them. We have seen this sort of humanitarian exception recently as the West rushed to gift democracy to the people of Iraq and Libya.

Certainly, the political structure depends very much upon this perception of ownership, since each government exists solely because it has the ability to dictate to the people within its boundaries how they live and behave. It claims the right to regularly and officially take as much of their money from them as it deems possible, and to borrow from the banks and the markets against the future productivity of the population. That this has to be done within some framework of law matters little when we see the speed with which basic laws safeguarding our freedom or setting our taxation are changed in order to pursue one political agenda after another.

> *The top gun, self-serving power structure*
> *Also claims outright ownership*
> *Of the lives of all those born*
> *Within their sovereignly claimed*
> *Geographical bounds*
> *And can forget their citizens' lives*
> *In their official warfaring*
> *Which, of psychological necessity*
> *Is always waged in terms*
> *Of moral rectitude*
> *While covertly protecting and fostering*
> *Their special self-interests.*
>
> Buckminster Fuller, 1895–1983, *Ethics: A Geoview*

17

Victimless Crimes

In Bolivia, a clown known only as "Mr. Twister" has been threatened with prison for refusing to promise a Santa Cruz court that he would not repeat his offence. Mr. Twister was charged with repeatedly feeding the parking meters of complete strangers.

The Guardian, June 1996

Nobody keeps track of how many billions are wasted worldwide every year trying to prevent members of the public from committing crimes without a victim, catching them when they do, processing them through courts, and securing them in overcrowded prisons thereafter. They have committed "crimes" that could harm no one but themselves, and often not even that. In some cases the prohibition is justified by a risk that is lower than many permitted activities, from skiing and horseback riding to drinking in bars or eating at fast food outlets. Millions of lives are actually damaged simply because people are indulging in activities the state has deemed possibly dangerous or decidedly deviant, whether that's protesting in public without a permit; buying and selling unlicensed herbal medicines or unapproved mood-altering drugs; partaking in dangerous sports; enjoying illicit forms of sex; attending unlicensed parties; dancing or singing without a permit; exposing your body in public; changing religion in fundamentalist countries; exceeding the speed limit at 3 AM; and much more besides.

> *In a free society, how can you commit a crime against yourself?*
>
> Jesse Ventura, American politician, former wrestler, 1951–

The state has various ways to protect us from doing things that it thinks are not good for us. It can take our money away in fines, confiscate our property, put us in jail, get us fired or liquidate our business. Hell . . . there are even situations where it can kill you to protect you from yourself. Even the right to take your own life is an offense in most parts of the world. I have this mad image in my mind of a crouching policeman shouting "Don't jump or I'll shoot!" to a would-be suicidée about to leap from the window ledge of a high-rise.

The state, in the interests of governing the nation, has no right to pass laws supposedly protecting us from ourselves, or them from our criticism and protest. Their basic remit for existence is to protect us from others who would want to attack us, or steal the property we have fairly acquired through our own endeavors, or through gratitude or bequest. In fact, the state that should protect us now makes the largest attack on our property of all—the institutionalized appropriation of over half of the value we add to creation every year (see chapter 23). Much of this "stolen" wealth is then turned against us—literally used to attack us when we choose to explore or do or witness or create things that are a threat to no one but, perhaps, ourselves.

Many scientific studies over several decades have shown cannabis use itself to be harmless. In centuries of usage, there has not been a death laid at the door of this innocuous drug. Yet thousands are arrested and processed at great expense through courts and prisons for indulging in this happier and safer alternative to alcohol. The rapid growth in prison building in both America and Britain is fueled by drug cases—an attack by the state on its own citizens. Nearly two million Americans today are either in jail, on parole, or on probation for drug offenses, primarily non-violent. Jailing and confiscating the property of citizens (or their suppliers) who like to puff cannabis or take other drugs neither benefits their lives nor serves any need of society. According to studies, statistics, and most retired law enforcement officers, the War on Drugs has had little or no effect on overall consumption of illegal drugs in the US. Ironically, it is often easier to source drugs inside jail than outside of it.

> *The illegality of cannabis is outrageous, an impediment to full utilization of a drug which helps produce the serenity and insight, sensitivity and fellowship so desperately needed in this increasingly mad and dangerous world.*

> Carl Sagan, American cosmologist, 1934–1996

We are, quite simply, being denied the sovereignty of our own minds as many consciousness-altering drugs, natural and synthetic, are banned for the prime reason that they induce a genuine euphoria and an ability to glimpse what lies behind the mirrors and the smoke of our constructed society. Either that, or they threaten the profits of pharmaceutical companies pushing their patented drugs to relieve the depression and anxiety of those who find their lives confusing and/or meaningless. Anti-depressant drugs, with all their attendant risks, are the single most-prescribed medication in the US. The War on Drugs has served only to heighten levels of drug abuse, driving consumers to take more dangerous and addictive substances than those traditionally on offer. There is a chapter dedicated to this subject later, covering aspects of it that cannot be touched upon within a single paragraph.

In many parts of the civilized world, the UK and America included, a permit is required to sing or dance in a public place. In the UK, for example, a license is required to play live music in a public establishment. An unlicensed venue that allowed a few customers to spontaneously break into song and dance could risk losing its right to trade. What kind of a crime is this? What kind of state thinks we need this kind of looking after?

People have been imprisoned, harassed, and had their children taken into state care because they rejected the official educational system approved by the state. Presumably the future of their children, as productive members of society, might be jeopardized if the state did not legislate just what they should all learn. Why should the state treat the rejection of their public education system as such a threat? It could be argued that the official educational system, with its centrally standardized curricula, does not always make for a very difficult example to beat. Educational standards in countries such as England and the United States are regularly exceeded by so-called Third World countries. Our own culture is filled with stories of peasants and uneducated immigrants who ended up magnates. Today, many people still rise to the top in their careers without having had any official schooling in their chosen arena.

> *Education is an admirable thing, but it is well to remember from time to time that nothing that is worth knowing can be taught.*
>
> Oscar Wilde, Irish writer, poet, and playwright, 1854–1900

The state has come to see itself as more responsible for your child than you. And if the state decides you are not being a good enough parent, then the state, the ultimate parent, will step in and take over, forcibly removing children from "unfit" parents. Though we regularly read of the abuse and assaults upon children in state-run homes and of these homes' magnetic attraction to pedophiles and sadists, state-supported abusers of children are rarely raided by the social services. The cases only seem to come to light after many years of bureaucratic obstructions and cover-ups and high-profile exposés in the press. Then broad inquiries are held, rarely resulting in any prosecution of the perpetrators, who may well by then have died of natural causes. In the UK the cost of keeping a child in state care averages £200,000 per year, six times the cost of sending them to an elite private school. Despite this cost, according to the Children's Society in 2012, the police estimate that some ten thousand children a year go missing from the care system altogether, which is not far short of the number taken into care each year. It makes you wonder.

Sex, our primary means of producing children, is another arena in which the state thinks it necessary to protect us from ourselves. Whether in print, film, the market, or the bedrooms of consenting adults, sex is regulated the world over by laws deemed to be for our own good. Many authors have been jailed and censured for writing about the joys of the basic natural mechanism that ensures the survival of our species. A similar fate has met publishers, filmmakers, and performers seeking to include sex in their subject matter. Conversely, those human acts that damage our species can be freely written about, or portrayed in print or films that graphically depict murder, injury, and destruction. What is so wrong with sex, that the depiction of it in print or film must be so controlled by law? Is it not curious that "sex and violence" are so often joined together when people are in a condemning mood, considering the opposite ends of the spectrum at which they exist? One creates life and the other destroys it.

Varying volumes of law and regulation still exist throughout the world, dictating what consenting adults may or may not do for pleasure, within the privacy of their own homes. Some of these prohibit consenting adults from having sex with those of the same gender, using orifices prohibited by law, being over-exposed in public, or indulging in painful and strange sexual activity. Some of the stranger and darker sexual practices may well have been caused by the repression and suppression of more "natural" tendencies earlier in life. Do we really need to have a government legislating what is acceptable for people to do with their own bodies, for their own pleasure? If society or a local culture chooses to shun or reject people because of their chosen lifestyle or sexual tendencies, then it will. But we should not endure a situation in which the state is empowered to harass and imprison such people—or indeed legislate their mandatory acceptance in your spare room B&B. The natural rhythms of society should be relied upon to eventually work this stuff out.

There is nothing to fear from those who seek to live their own lives outside the currently legislated norms of society, as long as they are not encroaching upon the freedom of others. If someone's choice is to live in a homemade tent in the woods without the benefit (and ecological cost) of hot and cold running water, central heating, and a flush toilet, then who are we or the state to say that this constitutes an illegal dwelling? Who are we to treat such people like criminals? The faulty thinking process that guides the state when enforcing their regulations imagines that if one person steps out of line then everybody will, altering the status quo. I encountered this very attitude when a beautifully painted fractal pavement appeared in front of my newly opened shop, Strange Attractions, which was devoted to chaos theory. Within two days workmen from the council arrived to dig it all up and lay down new gray paving. When guerrilla artist Howie Cooke asked the bureaucrat in charge "Why?" the official first complimented Howie on his work, then expressed his fears that if they allowed this, "it would lead to total chaos." Meanwhile two burnt-out abandoned cars littered the same road for two months, endangering children and looking pretty ugly. I contemplated starting an urban "terrorist" group after this, which would have gone out in the dead of night to paint pretty pictures around dangerous potholes in the road.

This state's obsession with maintaining the status quo fails to recognize that most people like toilets and television, plumbing, power, and many of the other conveniences of life. Everybody is not going to run out and live in a tree or a tent on common ground if the government stops arresting and harassing anyone who does. But those who did so of choice would certainly reduce their need for state assistance, housing stock, and ever more infrastructure.

> *Bureaucracy defends the status quo long past the time when the quo has lost its status.*
>
> Laurence J. Peter, devised the Peter Principle, 1919–1990

There are countless examples of the state's obsession with our private lives and businesses and how we live them and run them. At the core of it all is the assumption that the state knows best: that given the resources (*our* resources), they are better able to direct our lives than are we. Of course, since all the state knows is the status quo, the bulk of its regulation will be directed at maintaining the state's view of what the current culture constitutes. Many of the people who society views as cultural heroes—the great artists, musicians, thinkers, philosophers, and inventors of history—were, in their day, imprisoned, ridiculed, and harassed for their ideas and actions.

In addition to volumes of law that supposedly protect us from ourselves or others, we have a growing mountain of laws designed to mandate our compliance with government demands. There is no real victim involved in these crimes, and they have grown most of all in the US. The forfeiture laws of America, and now the UK, were initially brought in to fight "the drug menace" and are increasingly being extended to many other areas deemed criminal. The first extension was into banking, where all cash transactions above a certain threshold or so are classed as suspicious, with clerks and employees earning rewards by reporting such transactions. The owner of the money then risks having it forfeited—until and unless they can produce the records proving that their money arose from a legitimate, tax-paid transaction. An immigrant community leader returning to her native Vietnam with just over $10,000 of locally collected charitable contributions had it confiscated at a Los Angeles airport and suffered a further fine for non-completion of a simple reporting form. There was no suggestion that other laws were broken, or that anything illicit was involved.

Forfeiture law was extended in the 1990s to private doctors in the US, accelerating the move by doctors from private practice to health companies. It was deemed a criminal offense to make any clerical error in a patient's records, such as a wrong date or diagnosis code. Though the law was ostensibly brought in to help prevent fraud against insurance companies, there is no need for the error to have any fraudulent or medical consequences. During the law's first year of operation, in 1997, over $1 billion in assets was taken by the government from doctors who had neither had a trial nor been proved to have done anything damaging or malicious.

Police departments across America now budget annually for forfeiture revenue, targeting how much cash, goods, and property they will seize from the public each year. Their focus is shifting from solving or preventing crime to seizure of assets. Their innovative new techniques now mean that 80 percent of assets seizures are unaccompanied by any criminal prosecution. One such technique is the "reverse sting" in which an undercover cop poses as a drug dealer offering to sell to an unsuspecting buyer. As soon as the buyer produces a wallet, any money on him or her is legally seized, with no time-consuming charges having to be made.

Police love the drug war, because the forfeiture laws it inspired allow them to seize and keep private property with impunity. Corrupt cops get fabulous bribes, and corruption therefore runs rampant.

Robert Higgs, American economic historian, 1944–

It was not that long ago that racists were running South Africa and the southern states of the US. They passed laws making it illegal to express sentiments about black people being anything other than an inferior race. Today we have come full circle, and the law in many nations will fine or jail us for saying anything critical based upon somebody's race (or religion or sexuality in many places). Is it not strange that we can cruelly insult a person any way we like, calling them a bastard, an asshole, or somebody who has sex with their mother, yet if we precede that insult with "black" or "queer," then we have crossed an uncrossable line? Will it soon be illegal to call anybody baldie or fatty or gray or ugly?

Do we need the state to enact laws preventing us from speaking our thoughts, even when they are in conflict with the socially accepted norm? Those social norms are best shaped by allowing people to freely express their thoughts. The courageous blacks and whites who oposed apartheid and segregation in South Africa and the US had to risk jail and police beatings for speaking their minds. We are community animals and able to look after how we relate to each other without regulations dictating how or whether we express our thoughts. Some people are just bigoted misguided jerks with no respect for those of other cultures, sexual inclinations, or religions—and I want to know who they are! Let them expose their opinions to the public glare and become victims of public opinion, rather than classify recipients of their insults as victims. Let freedom flow.

> *What is ominous is the ease with which some people go from saying that they don't like something to saying that the government should forbid it. When you go down that road, don't expect freedom to survive very long.*
>
> Thomas Sowell, American economist
> and philosopher, 1930–

Although we are given the impression that our governments are aiming to selflessly look after the needs of the people, they are not comfortable when many of those people go out in the streets to express dissatisfaction with their service and activities. As a result, many nations of the world now demand that a license is granted for any protest, giving it official sanction while usefully identifying those responsible for the action. The state's cameramen will be out there in force too, making a record of all those who dare to be open about their grievance. This data harvesting can be and sometimes is used as an instrument to suppress all further expressions of discontent. In many nations of the world it is even worse, with mere criticism of the state or the supreme leader being enough to bring about fines, beatings, and imprisonment.

As we have seen, an increasing amount of today's law is not concerned with our protection at all, but with our conformity to government regulations and permitted behavior. I suggest that the ratio between these two types of laws could be used as an indicator of the degree to which any given state has tipped towards being termed "totalitarian."

This shift in attitudes towards the function of state policing of society is reflected in the changed terminology for US police, who once routinely referred to themselves as "peace officers" but changed this when it became a misnomer. They now call themselves "law enforcement officers," which is a more accurate term when we consider that much of their activity involves the forceful and often violent interruption of otherwise quite peaceful activity.

The whole concept of the victimless crime is at the heart of the breakdown of "law and order" so lamented by both citizens and politicians. Vast sums are spent, and armies of bureaucrats and police maintained, to ensure that we comply with needless regulations, primarily designed to keep things as the government would like them. This is the top-down control that so often blocks the natural evolution of our species. Of course these resources should be spent to stop real crime and its causes, but as long as the state is running things, it will be in the long-term interest of the prison industry to have more prisons and of the police service to have more crime.

Incarceration Rates around the World

COUNTRY	INMATES PER 100,000	
	1994*	2009*
United States	519	756
Russia	690	626
Ukraine	390	323
South Africa	368	334
Singapore	229	267
Romania	200	123
Hong Kong	179	143
England, Wales	93	150
China	xx	122
France	84	96
Germany	80	89
Turkey	80	142
Ireland	55	81
Japan	36	63
Cambodia	26	71
India	24	33

Note: Some of the figures may relate to the nearest year for which data were available.

In light of the above figures, it becomes more apparent why the US paints itself in the image of global policeman. Many American aid grants and commercial permits require that recipients and trade partners enforce various laws designed to spread a global morality molded on "the American way." It reminds us of the arrogance of Christian missionaries putting clothes on natives lest they be corrupted by their own nakedness. The numbers above show good potential for the export of prison technology to all those countries less diligent at enforcing and multiplying their laws. At those international prison industry conventions, they must be drooling over the prospect of locking up millions of chillum-smoking sadhus breaking cannabis laws in India. The US and UK now take pride in training police and paramilitary forces all over the world in the newest techniques of civilian surveillance and crowd control, at the same time selling them equipment needed to spy upon and "manage" their populations.

18

Poverty and Crime: A Popular Myth

Nepalese vendor of used flashlight parts.

It has almost become an accepted truth in the Western world today that poverty is one of the fundamental causes of crimes against property—crimes that have victims. That this is both untrue and baseless becomes obvious with but a moment's reflection on the situation. Crime stems not from a lack of wealth but from a lack of morality, and there is little to suggest that morality is the exclusive preserve of or even a natural consequence of being "poor." It is an insult to the financially lacking, who constitute a majority of the world's population, to suggest that immorality is created because of their lack of monetary wealth. Many of these communities indeed show far lower levels of crime than we experience in the West, and manage to lead richer lives than many a neurosis-ridden city dweller. We are indeed poverty stricken in the West, but not in the financial department. From the list of incarceration rates in the previous chapter, it is impossible to discern any connection between poverty and crime.

Poverty and crime are undoubtedly sometimes found in combination, fueling each other in locations like the favelas of Rio de Janeiro. But those who tear down the rainforest with government grants cannot plead poverty to excuse their crime—neither can those who destroy indigenous cultures by selling their land rights to mining companies. The idea of poverty breeding crime is ironic when we consider the global criminal activities that extremely wealthy people undertake in order to acquire even more wealth. Such greed led to the subprime mortgage crisis of 2008, bringing down the world's financial system. In 2009 the Bank of England created £200 billion pounds of new money out of thin air, as part of its "quantitative easing" policy to boost the economy. Did anybody notice? In other circumstances "printing money" is referred to as counterfeiting, considered a serious crime because it reduces the value of all the other money in circulation—stealing from everyone. By comparison, the total estimated cost of all other forms of crime in 2009 was under £100 billion.

In the Western world, we have suffered great periods of financial poverty such as the Great Depression of 1930, when people lived on their wits with no social net to protect them. Though many lost everything they had owned, and soup lines formed in the streets, levels of crime and murder did not soar to anything like today's record levels. Petty crimes of the unauthorized food consumption variety may have been higher, but a huge section of society did not lose their basic morality when they lost their money.

Bank robbers Bonnie and Clyde achieved fame because of their uniqueness—this kind of stuff did not happen often. They certainly did not rob that much, even adjusting for inflation. A widespread hatred of banks in the 1930s also boosted their legendary status. Though extremes of poverty and wealth existed in the so-called Wild West of nineteenth century America, the chance of being murdered or mugged or burgled was lower in many of these places than it is today. Bank and train robberies and shootouts were rare events remembered for years after. That gunfight at the OK Corral happened just once and went into legend. Jesse James was a one-off.

It is almost criminal how we trivialize our own value and wealth by insisting on such a linear scorecard. We end up totaling all the stuff that was sold for money in a particular geographical area, and dividing it by the number of humans living there, arriving thereby at the average "per capita" wealth of that country. I ask you, what about the wealth of good health, happiness, an unpolluted environment, fullness of love, friends, family, and a freedom from rules and regulation made and enforced by people with whom you have no connection?

> *No one would choose a friendless existence on condition of having all other things in the world.*

Aristotle, 384–322 BCE

I will argue that a rural Thailand peasant in a happy self-sufficient community, eating pure food and breathing clean air, free of debt, far removed from sources of pollution both environmental and mental, largely removed from bureaucracy, taxation, and regulation, is *in fact* a wealthier human being than is a deeply neurotic sales executive in New York who's unsure of his job security in a soul-destroying industry, and who financially earns perhaps one hundred times as much as our Thai peasant, but still not enough to meet his mortgage and loan repayments plus living expenses and child support. Maybe we need a few more words for different forms of poverty.

Unnecessary laws, prohibitions, and regulations, which are rigidly maintained by law enforcement officers, are patently one of the single greatest sources of crime in this world, not poverty. As you will understand from the rest of this book, they also discourage us from developing our own codes of morality and make it easier for criminals to view their crimes as thwarting the state and breaking its rules, rather than as committing an offense against the society to which the criminal belongs. The distinction is becoming dangerously blurred between what is a true crime against a fellow human and what is just transgressing a law that seeks to standardize behavior rather than protect any potential victims.

I used to think I was poor. Then they told me I was not poor, I was needy. They told me it was self-defeating to think of myself as needy, I was deprived. Then they told me underprivileged was overused. I was disadvantaged. I still do not have a dime but I have a great vocabulary.

Jules Feiffer, American humorist, 1929–

19

So What's News?

The press is the living jury of the nation.

James Gordon Bennett, newspaper editor, 1795–1872

The danger that the press may misunderstand or misinterpret or even misinform is in the final analysis a small price to pay compared to the services the news media render when they expose wrongdoing or gross errors of judgment by the powers that be.

Leonard H. Marks, lawyer, 1916–1990

Our mainstream daily news is regularly dominated by the plans, programs, proposals, and political battles of politicians—or by the failures, collapse, dashed hopes, wars, and scandals resulting from the plans, programs, and proposals reported in years gone by. Election contests are a regular feature in the news, even those in which it will make little difference who wins. Next time you look at a newspaper or watch the news, take note of how much is concerned with the above. It is only the names and the places, the numbers and the tools, the sparks and the ideologies, that change from month to month, year to year, century to century. They really ought to call it "The Olds," though it can, of course, be terribly new for those who are not reading about violent conflicts from a comfortable distance.

The news provides us with an ever-changing window on how those who think they run the planet spend vast sums of our money by attempting to maintain and manipulate the status quo at home, or forcibly imposing a new status quo upon a foreign nation. In relatively recent years, the idea of centrally managing the status quo has resulted in a proliferation of endless strictures as to what is and is not a house, a car, an eating apple, a permitted state of mind, a legal gathering, permissible sex, safe enough for idiots, and other matters large and small. When states disagree with one another, our propaganda machines churn out the news about rebels and insurgents, freedom fighters and terrorists, allies and enemies, with the roles regularly reversing. Wars and other forms of state-on-state conflict always make essential news content in our conflict-obsessed culture.

Though the news is dominated by the repetitive and confrontational activities of politicians and the state, it seems clear the most valuable and lasting positive changes to our culture arise from people, not politicians. In fact, the world's politicians seem to do the same old thing over and over again—which is to tell us what to do and beat us over the head if we don't listen. Their arguments with each other too often lead to fights and more sad news stories about innocent bystanders (people quite like us with babies, hearts, families, feelings, and so on) getting beat over the head (i.e., bombed, shelled, jailed, or shot). Amazingly, there is still room left for relevant and important and sometimes uplifting news, as well as all the engrossing mush of celebrity lives and competitive sports.

Despite its tendency to fill our heads with all the world's anguish and grief, a free media can perform an invaluable service for society and does a better job of monitoring and exposing the abuses and iniquities of our world than does the "protective" state. How often have we witnessed the government being the last to acknowledge its own corruption and abuse, and then only after revelation in the media? The media is often the first to inform us of scandals involving large or small corporations and dangers facing us through exposure to environmental chemicals or diseases in the food chain. Were we relying solely on government bulletins, we would know little of oil spills in the oceans, corruption in government, rising asthma among children, Mad Cow Disease, nuclear radiation leaks, Gulf War syndrome, the disappearing ozone hole, or endangered species.

A free press can, of course, be good or bad, but, most certainly without freedom, the press will never be anything but bad.

Albert Camus, Nobel Prize-winning author and
philosopher, 1913–1960

The media provides us with radio and TV programs dedicated to airing consumer grievances against companies, providing negative advertising for businesses, and warning us off that company and its faulty products. Consumer magazine *Which?* began publishing in 1957 and is still going strong, despite the wide range of dedicated product or service review websites to be found online, which are commonly free. I sought out such a site myself, in order to get even by publicizing my own appalling experience with a chain of lodges for travelers. I found that most of the comments on the site gave them the minimum 1 out of 5 rating, with many describing accounts even more appalling than my own. I wish I'd checked that site beforehand, but regularly do so now before booking accommodation. We live and learn.

Media has evolved through the chaos of our developing culture and technology, making full use of the once inconceivable capacity to send information across the world in a moment. People on the streets with smartphones have become instant video reporters for the established media, and are increasingly creating a new media. In those nations where the mainstream media has lost its capacity for great investigative journalism, the void is being filled with an abundance of revealing information published on the Internet or dispersed through social networks. We do need to exercise our bullshit filters a little more often than is needed with mainstream media, but as with mainstream media we come to trust and respect some sources more than others.

Ultimately, when independent and free, our mainstream media will deliver news about which we wish to be informed; if our preference is for conflict, celebrity news, or innovative discovery, then that is what we will receive. However, information technology has made it possible for many of us to bypass traditional media and create our own network of information sharing that is both free and independent. The news has come a long way from the town crier of long ago, proclaiming announcements dictated by the state. We can only guess at where this will take us in ten years, or rather where we will take it—for the media is increasingly being shaped from the bottom up, by we the people.

> *. . . Were it left to me to decide whether we should have a government without newspapers or newspapers without government, I should not hesitate a moment to prefer the latter.*
>
> Thomas Jefferson, American Founding Father, 1743–1826

20

The State of Business

Little resembling a free market remains in most of those major nations that built their greatness on the free market and then regulated it out of reach to those without degrees, certificates, and bank loans. Letting your child go out on the street selling lemonade today (as I did when a boy) might easily result in the toddler being taken into care. We are not free to turn our home into a restaurant or herbal treatment clinic, and require a license or permit to sell anything in a public place. Where a semblance of the free market survives, it thrives, in farmers markets and flea markets, car boot and yard sales, eBay and Craigslist and Silk Road.

The structure of the so-called free market is both determined and distorted by the state's involvement. The roots of this abberation lie in the core need of the state to raise as much money in taxation as possible—regardless of how, where, or from whom it is taken; regardless of where and on what it is spent. As Jean Baptiste Colbert, finance minister to Louis XIV in the seventeenth century, so eloquently put it: "The art of taxation consists in so plucking the goose as to obtain the largest possible amount of feathers with the smallest possible amount of hissing." Forget all the propaganda about social engineering and wealth redistribution.

Large corporations make taxation much easier for the state by removing tax from what we have earned before we even get a chance to see it, let alone do anything rash like spend it. How much easier it is to dip into one pot to collect from two thousand employees than to rely on two thousand people to account for themselves once a year and "pay what is due." Far less hissing. The state loves the simplicity of dealing with one big unit, whether in collecting taxes or enforcing compliance with state regulation. Yet the vast majority of innovation and evolution comes from small business at the free and flexible end of free enterprise, which regulation rarely favors.

A short-term attitude pervades modern business ethics because of the penalty the tax man applies to taking a long-term view of how you wish to manage the assets of your own or your shareholders' business. When profit is not shifted to head office tax havens, or disbursed quickly on new equipment or expansion of the business, a painfully large chunk of it gravitates towards the taxman. Just a century ago companies all over the world used to keep most of their profits, sometimes piles of profits. Even after paying for the big houses, jewelry, and servants, there was a lot left over. With it they made long-term investments in the original infrastructure of canals, railways, communication lines (across land and sea), underground transport systems, power generation and distribution, bridges, and more. They spent their own money and if the project failed, it cost them and not the taxpayer. They also set up and funded numerous universities and social institutions. Today, most big projects in the private sector involve significant levels of bank financing, with the emphasis on earning rapid returns more so than on long-term investment.

The real costs to our species and its enterprises occasioned by state interference in the feedback loop are incalculable. We are community animals and good at sorting things out from the bottom up. It may take longer to fix some problems from within, but when we do the fixes are more durable. Natural feedback loops are the mechanisms that keep our world in balance, with constant adjustment to circumstance. The state replaces feedback loops with laws and directives dreamt up by those who believe they know where we should be headed, creating legislation to force us in that direction rather than risking letting it happen naturally. Lawmakers' thoughts are often influenced by industry lobbyists, which can result in the passing of laws and regulation making possible activities that the natural feedback loop would have ruled out—nuclear power and GM foods are prime examples.

What are some of the damaging twists in the feedback loop that the coercive state has visited upon us? A few examples:

Limited liability is a distortion of natural human enterprise, which the state thinks is a benefit to society. Perhaps wealthy businessmen talked them into it. Except for in monastic communities, the concept did not exist at the beginning of the nineteenth century and came into legislation during the middle of it. Simply put, limited liability (indicated by Ltd, LLC, or PLC after the company name) makes it legal to break commitments and walk away from the mess you have created, provided you did it according to the book. This is possible because, by government permission, you are allowed to be a "limited liability company" instead of a person or a group of people interacting with the rest of the world. Since time immemorial, governments have walked away from their messes, and limited liability makes it all right for businesses to do so too. To hold this status, a company agrees to follow the state's rules of good business practice, submitting audited accounts, annual reports, and records of shareholder meetings.

The benefit of limiting liability is that it enables thousands of small investors to become mini-owners of a large company over which they have no effective operational control. By knowing that whatever happens to the company, they will never be called upon to cover any massive unforeseen loss or damage, they invest more readily, and may do so with a less urgent concern for the legality or morality of the business operation.

Society never developed such a mechanism as limited liability on its own, but it did develop insurance, which can and does cover against the liability of accidentally poisoning a customer, a whole community, or having your factory burn down. Insurance ensures that a company is able to honor its commitments, even if its ship, real or proverbial, sinks. With few exceptions, we work as a society by honoring and being responsible for our debts and commitments, exercising compassion when the situation calls for it. Why should companies be exempt from this, and the extra dimension of responsible investors and prudent management that accompanies full responsibility?

You might agree that if I convince you my brand of shampoo, which in truth makes your hair fall out, is actually best for your hair, then I have a liability to do more than just return your money. However, with limited liability, I can be so incompetent that I accidentally sell thousands of bottles of this depilatory shampoo and end up with thousands of customers who want their money back, plus a costly wig. I've been keeping and filing the right stuff, but don't have adequate insurance, or enough money in the pockets of my limited liability company. The only option is to call in the liquidator, drive back to my country house in the 4x4, lounge by the swimming pool, and ponder what to do next. You don't even get your money back. Of course, when this sort of abuse occurs, we clamor to have the government legislate precise new standards for hair shampoo to safeguard our scalps in the future. Luckily for us, most people making hair shampoo recognize that happily hirsute customers make them more money in the long term—and have insurance just in case.

Ironically, the state further compounds the immoral protection of limited liability not only by making it available but also by posing the greatest threat from which the individuals operating any company would wish to be protected. The vast majority of companies forced into receivership are pushed there because of unpaid taxes, often ones that they are commanded to collect on behalf of the government, such as the VAT (value added tax) applied throughout the European Union. And those taxes are collected from whatever is left of a company's assets before the remainder is allocated to banks, creditors, and unfulfilled or hairless customers.

Taxation itself has other hidden side effects, apart from siphoning wealth out of the system and encouraging short-term thinking. Many large companies and wealthy individuals expend considerable resources and set up complicated protection schemes, which lock up money in offshore havens that might otherwise have been reinvested in the local environment. This is an artificially stimulated loss to the community. Moreover, all that top brainpower devoted to this effort is a waste of human intellect, which would better be applied to figuring out ways to use resources more efficiently, improve working standards, develop clean power, and adapt to climate change. You get the idea.

Because we take it for granted, it is difficult to conceive the size of the impact that taxation has on the basic running of a business. Tax can often be the single greatest cost passed on to the consumer purchasing products or services. The tax accumulates with import duties, excise taxes, employee taxes, business rates, value added tax, benefits in kind tax, and a whole host of money-grabbing mechanisms around the world. Then, if that business manages to take in more money than it spends (makes a profit), a further chunk is taken in corporation tax. That businesses spend a lot of time considering the tax implications of their activities and means of reducing the overall impact on product cost is understandable. The unfortunate effect of this is a diversion from the actual remit of a business, which is to serve its customers, and a substantial added-on cost to almost every product we consume.

The state depends on big business to implement its relentless taxation of the individual, something that has been instinctively resisted by many generations of individuals before us. If you were relying on other people's earnings to support yourself, wouldn't you prefer to tax those people's incomes through a single employer, rather than have to deal with that many machine operators, sales assistants, hairdressers, market traders, newsagents, builders, gardeners, masseurs, and wandering minstrels? I think so, and it is no accident, nor in the interests of the general public, that government policy has for many years encouraged the growth of large faceless corporate culture.

Business rates, health & safety regulation, parking restrictions, usage licenses, and many other measures make today's retailing environment increasingly hostile to anyone other than large corporations with large resources. The ever-changing bodies of regulation and the requirements of accounting for taxation place such burdens on anyone seeking to "do business" as an individual that effectively, most are weeded out. Many people could run a small venture with ease if freed from the need to keep specific records determined by the needs of the taxman, while keeping abreast of all the changing regulations, and collecting tax on the tax authorities' behalf. It need not be so difficult to find a way of fitting into our society and providing a useful service or product to others. We are naturally very good at doing this using nothing more than our instincts. I have seen happy ten-year-olds on the beaches of India selling clothes and handiwork to tourists, in five different languages.

The online business environment, not in evidence at all during the first incarnation of this book, has once again opened wide the gate to the small entrepreneur who need only get his or her head around something as simple as eBay and PayPal. I suspect the tax collectors are working hard at developing a means to collect taxes on all those now relatively free Internet exchanges between people. Of course the large corporate retailers will already be charging and paying taxes on everything they sell online and thus supporting any legislation to make it a "level playing field." Those collectors just have to figure out how to keep the "hissing" from being too loud, perhaps by starting with a small transaction tax, which slowly escalates. We will see.

Government schemes create another major distortion of the natural evolution of business in society. These are designed to protect and promote certain industries—even when they are outdated and delivering overpriced product. Nuclear power was developed for one purpose alone—to supply material for the state's nuclear weapons. It does not make economic sense and is uninsurable. Not even the most notorious industrialist of the nineteenth century would have jeopardized his entire wealth on such a risk. What company could cover the loss of a city the size of Tokyo or London, the re-location of its residents, and their medical bills for life? That responsibility falls upon the state, and we must wonder whether they will be able to cover it. We now know that the evacuation of Tokyo was considered after Fukushima, and have been told that, if all goes well, it will take over forty years to clean up the mess and stabilize the dangerously damaged reactors.

Billions are still squandered by the EU's Common Agricultural Policy because the thought of dismantling it is too shocking for the bureaucrats who make a living perpetuating its depredations. Environmentally damaging and economically questionable dam projects are pursued in developing nations, because the money has been donated by Western states eager to secure lucrative contracts for their friends in business. Roads are often built for the sake of budget fulfillment, using the handy state mechanism of compulsory purchase to overcome any natural opposition by homeowners refusing to sell what they rightfully own. Objectors are arrested or hauled out by bailiffs. England's Department of Trade and Industry's budget in 1993–1994 was £3,600,000,000, to be spent helping British industry be more competitive at home and abroad. Imagine how much more competitive these businesses would have been had that £3.6 billion not been removed from their earnings and their customers' pockets in the first place. (I was unable to find more recent figures but the point remains the same.)

> Millions of pounds of public money have been pumped into funding dozens of British films that have never been shown in any cinema.

> Sunday Times, July 1997

Regulation is often cited by businesses bemoaning the costs of unnecessary compliance. They are often justified since much government regulation of business is out of date or inappropriate to the situation. It is more often confrontational than cooperative. Very few businesses would actually survive if they did comply with all the regulation directed at them. Despite all the regulations, when negligent errors are made, the state-imposed consequences are usually inappropriate and focused on fines rather than compensation for the victims. Today's big pharmaceutical companies routinely budget for hundreds of millions of dollars in fines each year to cover that part of their deceptive practice and negligence that is discovered.

A common example of regulation gone mad is the state's widely derided obsession with our protection, manifested by health & safety regulation. I first encountered this in the 1970s when running Harmony/Whole Earth Foods, a natural food company making and packing yummy planet-friendly products. Often, the packaging equipment we purchased needed to be altered to make it workable, and we had to remove the state-imposed safeguards in order to operate it. Now this madness has grown and extended to our homes and parks and playgrounds. Millions of tons of perfectly good food are discarded to ensure that nobody ever need use their eyes, nose, or taste buds to check for edibility, as we have done for thousands of years. It goes on. Considering the extremes to which H&S reaches into our lives, it is astounding that we are still permitted to indulge in the clearly hazardous activity of inserting an object with four sharp points into our mouths dozens of times every day. At the very least, we should be barred from watching screens, reading newspapers, or carrying on a conversation while undertaking fork usage. Will the day ever come when metal forks require cheek guards and eye protectors?

He who seeks to regulate everything by law is more likely to arouse vices than to reform them. It is best to grant what cannot be abolished, even though it be in itself harmful. How many evils spring from luxury, envy, avarice, drunkenness and the like, yet these are tolerated because they cannot be prevented by legal enactments.

Baruch Spinoza, Dutch philosopher and scientist,
1632–1677

We already rely on standards and regulations that are effective and flexible and so invisible that we can easily fail to appreciate them. On a simple level, it was Heinz that set the original standard for baked beans and Bic that did so for disposable cigarette lighters. Not an awful lot has changed since they did so—with no state regulation required, aside from the little sticker on each lighter warning you not to eat it, ignite it inside your nose, or put it in the crib with baby (or something like that). Many trades form societies to set standards for registered members so that the consumer can avoid uninsured architects or untrained acupuncturists.

State protection is a poor substitute for consumer awareness, though it would be comforting to think that you didn't have to concern yourself with too much detailed monitoring when out buying and selling things in the free market. Fairtrade International led the way as an independent stamp of ethical quality, as the Soil Association set a standard for Earth-friendly organic farming. This author looks forward to much more of this independent oversight, and must slip in that the very first Fairtrade certified product was Green & Black's Maya Gold chocolate, from the company founded by my brother Craig and his wife Josephine.

False Legitimacy is often extended to businesses that would otherwise have neither the means nor any reason to exist. As mentioned earlier, this is patently the case with nuclear power, a dangerous and uneconomic activity that would never merit its existence in a free economy. Unless exonerated by the state, companies have responsibility under common law for their activities. Nuclear power companies do not take responsibility for obsolete plants that will remain toxic and need minding for many tens of thousands of years beyond their thirty- to forty-year working lifespan. No insurance company is willing to cover for the incalculable potential costs of nuclear accidents, as demonstrated at Three Mile Island, Chernobyl, and Fukushima. The state will attempt to underwrite any disaster repairs, with our money. If I keep referring to nuclear, it is because nothing else on this planet matches its potential to so permanently destroy virtually all of this beautiful thing called life.

The principle and practice of artificial fertilization of the soil with nitrogen and phosphates metaphorically exploded with Uncle Sam's efforts after World War II to find another use for the outputs of America's giant munitions industry. The similar chemical composition of explosives and fertilizer makes it easy for terrorists to convert the one to the other. It now seems apparent that decades of artificially boosting crop yields with chemical fertilizers has led to weaker food crops with less resistance to insects, fungi, and weeds. This weakened food crop now requires regular dosing with an ever-stronger arsenal of chemical poisons to keep the competition at bay.

Genetically modified foods are made possible by the state; each product on sale has been officially approved by the government, who thereby assume the responsibility for any downstream consequences that may arise. As Phil Angell, Monsanto's director of corporate communications, concisely put it: "Monsanto should not have to vouchsafe the safety of biotech food. Our interest is in selling as much of it as possible. Assuring its safety is the FDA's job." (*New York Times,* October 25, 1998).

We are fighting a war against the land that feeds us, undermining the natural mechanisms with which it works its magic in our mechanistic attempt not to feed the world, but to feed the world cheap meat, supply cheap ingredients to the food processing industry, and make big bucks for the agribusiness lobby. The enormous hidden costs of the state-supported cheap food policy are becoming apparent, as rivers and oceans are polluted by agricultural runoff and medical facilities strained by those suffering from diet-related allergies, degenerative diseases, antibiotic-resistant pathogens, and a rising tide of obesity. Ironically, food isn't even cheap any more, with prices rising as the cost of farm chemicals increases and climate change wreaks havoc on the growing seasons.

The vast bulk of the global arms industry is made legitimate by one customer alone—the state or would-be state—and is the primary recipient of aid monies earmarked for "defense." Here is an international industry manufacturing products that are designed to destroy large numbers of human beings at once, often in gruesome and painful ways, and it is considered respectable and legitimate! How crazy is that? This artificially stimulated industry makes products that cost us even more when they are used (there is a chapter devoted to this industry in this book).

Many poorly considered international aid projects are carried out at huge cost, locked into conditions attached to aid money that ensure most of its return to businesses within the donor state. Both Iraq and Afghanistan are littered with incomplete school, hospital, and infrastructure building projects. Most of these activities, and many other enterprises that waste rather than return our effort, or return a short-term economic benefit at great long-term cost, would not be in existence without the false legitimacy accorded by the coercive states dishing out the money.

Finally (for the purposes of this chapter, not for lack of examples), the state's pervasive regulation and control of business has the effect of stifling the enterprise of our species. This makes it increasingly difficult for an individual with a bright idea to go into business, or even someone with any old idea for that matter. An early insight into this restrictive climate came to me some years ago at a cafe in Marrakech, where I noticed a young man standing on the corner each evening with a pack of twenty cigarettes, selling them singly to passersby. The customers were able to better manage their habit by buying the cigarettes singly. The young man was able to set up his own business as a retailer for the cost of a pack of cigarettes—an almost inconceivable concept in our developed "free" democracy. The bridge is great between the skills we need to manage our own enterprise, and those needed to do so according to the requirements of the state. Many are unable to cross this bridge, despite having all the skills that nature demands to interact in this way with society.

Companies and those engaged in business do need to take responsibility for their activities and for the wider costs of their operations. We as a society, including those businesses, need to develop means for this to happen. I suggest that without the oppressive and invasive interference by the state in the regular day-to-day transactions of mankind (which we call enterprise or business), the mechanisms to provide this wider responsibility would have evolved in the natural course of events. We cannot know how the widespread trade guilds and associations that arose in medieval Europe would have evolved had their regulating roles not been subsumed by the growing state. We are not going to make business more responsible by giving up this responsibility to the state, thereby putting a stop to its natural development in a feedback-connected environment.

Indeed, one of the disturbing developments of modern times is the ongoing attempt by large multinational corporations to manipulate and actually govern the mechanism of the state. Of course, this could be seen in perspective as just the latest arrival in a long chain of command—including but not limited to kings, pharaohs, senates, emperors, churches, dynasties, generals, presidents, and parliaments. So why not multinationals? Why not—because coercion is not and never has been an effective tool for determining our culture's evolutionary path, whoever has their hands on the coercive tiller. Multinational corporations are no more able to effectively dictate evolution than are democratically elected parliaments, the Church, or those with the most guns. But those seeking power and influence will always be striving to get their hands upon the controls of the state. Can you blame them, really?

> *There is nothing so useful to man in general, nor so beneficial to particular societies and individuals, as trade. This is that alma mater, at whose plentiful breast all mankind are nourished.*
>
> Henry Fielding, English novelist and dramatist, 1707–1754

21

Global Corporation, Inc.

We are right, of course, to beware a nightmare world run by corporations, controlling our minds with advertising, filling our lives with material junk, and devastating our Earth in their eternal quest for a fast buck. The most frightening manifestation of this is the faceless multinational, plying its trade with tentacles in every country of the world, often manipulating local laws to its own benefit. Some of these companies will sell products with known health risks in markets where they are still legally declared safe. We hear of healthy mothers in Africa being told that formula feed is healthier for their babies than their own milk. Large cola companies have purchased the local competition and pumped their own product into regional markets. Even in the highly regulated food chain of the US, we find inadequately tested GM food slipped, unlabeled, into the supply chain; damaging artificial sweeteners approved; and a hormone fed to dairy cows that is banned in most of the world. How can we expect our humble interests to be well protected by a state that harvests so much of its main product, our earned wealth, through the agency of large corporations?

People have been doing business together, trading, or whatever you want to call it, stretching back beyond written history. Some get together and form companies, and if they're good at it, they grow and prosper. We are justly distressed by the behavior of some large corporations when we see them lobbying the state for restrictive regulations; paying it for the mineral rights to ancient and sacred tribal lands; or arranging for its police to arrest, beat, or shoot protestors or striking workers. Most of today's corporate lobbying is little more than institutionalized bribery. There undoubtedly have been, and will be, instances of shocking and immoral corporate behavior without resort to using the state's agencies, but it is not the norm. Far be it for me to cite McDonalds as an example, but it did not get to be the world's biggest burger brand by snuffing out the competition or by any devious activity. At its origins, McDonalds was an honorably operated company with burgers, french fries, and milkshakes that were above average, consistent, and speedily delivered.

Some companies will shift direction, merge with others, and grow large, while we see other entire industries wither and die, with video rental shops becoming as redundant as the flint knappers who were once a vital part of the arms industry. Wikipedia is the world's biggest information source, Google its primary search engine. We can no more denounce a large corporation for the sake of its size than we can the Rolling Stones on account of their disproportionately large following. On a genuinely free and less-lumpy-if-not-level playing field, there might be less abuse and less scope for global domination of an industry by one player. It's a brave man who stands up for the corporate world in these difficult times, but I'm a brave man who did well in that world, doing good things and working with lots of great and very committed people. I was an upstart in 1982, launching this new product called the VegeBurger in a blaze of publicity that had the meat trade very concerned. During those burger years I met many in the meat trade and was secretly disappointed to find they were all pretty good people, by and large honest about what they were doing, and never displaying any malicious behavior towards me or my business. And when some were caught out with horsemeat in 2013, they were seriously damaged by it; the incidence will drop off substantially in future. Some of the brands may never recover consumer confidence unless they take positive steps to earn it back.

We already have an extensive network of business enterprises spanning continents. I see no way to get rid of them, and no sound rationale for doing so. Some of them are even rather good at what they do, taking oil from beneath stormy seas, transporting it to land, refining it, and delivering to our vehicle, for less than the cost of bottled water when the tax is deducted.

So you might as well get to know your local multinationals. They will continue to be a part of your future unless you choose to live off the grid, in which case they are not going to respond by sending out their killer drones—not only because you might be a customer of their solar panels, but also because with rare exceptions that is not how companies do business. There is an awful lot of shit piled upon business and it is often deserved. But unlike government, business frequently responds to a tarnished reputation by polishing up its act, instead of focusing upon capturing and imprisoning the whistleblower who tarnished it.

In these days of corporation bashing, it might be worthwhile to look at the much-maligned beast from a few different perspectives. Many multinationals now have sales greater than the GNP of most of the world's nation states. Despite the power this gives them, as they get even larger, they will be less and less likely to find a reason to rain bombs upon us, their global customers. This is so unlikely for any business that very few, if any, of today's multinationals have a special reserve of bombs or bullets stored away—just in case the need arises. This cannot be said of today's nation states.

Not many businesses will put you in jail, fine you, or harass you if you absolutely refuse to buy their product, however brilliantly clever the advertising you don't respond to, however many millions they spend promoting it, or however much they think they know you need it. There is a choice and even though a lot of people are "fighting it out" in the marketplace, rarely does anyone actually get maimed or killed. With footwear, for instance, we end up with a choice of shoes, sandals, slippers, sneakers, thongs, skis, roller blades, and boots. We have leather boots, rubber boots, canvas boots, space boots, and wading boots in all colors, sizes, and styles. And in most parts of the world, notwithstanding the varieties of footwear available and the size of the industry, it is still perfectly legal to go barefoot.

It is not unusual for business to respond quickly to consumer needs and demands, especially when a well-publicized scandal is involved, or a new market is perceived. Large companies can be slow to respond, turning with the speed of a giant supertanker, but they can and do eventually react to the pressure of their customers. They certainly spend many millions in research intended to anticipate consumer wants. Smaller, more flexible companies respond more quickly to changing trends, sometimes initiating them. When they do this, they can grow faster, steal an edge on the competition, and make more money—thus getting bigger. It's a moving picture. But without state collusion, neither large nor small companies can force us to purchase a product that most of us demonstrably do not want—such as the fluoridation of our water supply, or unjustified foreign wars.

Companies usually stop short of killing or imprisoning their competition and critics. Even that early multinational, IBM, which effectively controlled the world computing market in the early 1970s, could only stand by and watch while two young nerds in a California garage changed the world of computing with the introduction of Apple's first computer. Apple added two brand new features to computing: screens and keyboards. Hello personal computers, goodbye magnetic tapes and trained operators. IBM's chairman had predicted in 1949 that the number of computers in the world would eventually reduce to just five. Steve Jobs and Steve Wozniak thought everybody should have one and made that their business. One of their little Apple IIe's was core to my emergent VegeBurger empire during the early 80s, doing all the hard work with me from the spare bedroom, in what would later be termed a virtual company.

Many big businesses got to be where they are today by starting small with a brilliant new product that enriched all of our lives in one way or another. Other small companies got big by responding to consumers' changing desires faster than the established giants of their industry. Some get big by shaping those desires, or even by creating new things to desire that have never been imagined before. In the vast new frontier of cyberspace, fortunes are made and empires are built upon no more than a very clever idea. Our era's exploration and development of the Internet is akin to discovering the Americas anew, this time with no native population to exterminate and no Pacific Ocean to contain its expansion.

Few companies claim the right, or even harbor the desire, to break into your house at any time of day and night to ensure that you are not ingesting, reading, or watching something of which they disapprove. This even applies if you choose to watch some devastatingly revealing, dirt-digging video produced by a new startup company, whose stated aim is to put the brand leader right out of business. Even if you have been drinking Coke every day of your life for years, you can switch overnight to water, orange juice, or beer without so much as a veiled threat from the Coca-Cola company. The most they can do is buy the company that sells you the water. I was amused to see vending machines in the US offering a full selection of the Coca-Cola Corporation's soft drinks at one dollar each, and half liter bottles of water at two dollars. They're fighting back, and if people will pay money to drink water with a clean taste and without fluoride, then soft drink makers will swallow hard and figure out how to make a living doing it.

Many companies offer a guarantee with their product, so that if the promised washing machine never arrives or breaks down completely, you have an opportunity to correct the situation. The commercial principle and practice of offering guarantees existed long before legislation made it mandatory. You usually do get what you are promised and if there are, say, only four cans of beer in the six-pack, then you can actually point this out to the vendor and get some money refunded. Try doing that when the state promises us one thing and delivers another.

> *A business must have a conscience as well as a counting house.*
>
> Sir Montague Burton, the tailor, 1885–1952

The growing weight of overall taxation on business and its employees may well have reduced the level of backup service that the average consumer might expect to accompany a product purchase. I remember when my mother spilled some Copydex glue on our carpet in the 1950s. She wrote to the company asking for advice on how to remove it. Within twenty-four hours a local representative was at our doorstep with a bottle of the appropriate solvent and help with its application. Margaret Sams remained a loyal user of Copydex for the rest of her long life.

Businesses do quite commonly sack disgraced and dishonest executives. We occasionally read of this in the newspapers and rarely (banking excepted) find that the disgraced executives move on to greater and higher positions in the firms or are retired early for medical reasons with full pay. When internal corruption is discovered, it is quite common for those involved to be dismissed with no consideration at all. Sometimes corporate big shots may get an undeserved "golden handshake" if there are no legal grounds for their removal, but life will always have some warts.

Holding onto a monopoly in a free world is not as easy as you might think. While the government maintains the (one and only) Monopolies Commission to check abuses, there are few examples of a long and stable corporate monopoly that did not rely upon state support and legislation. Few "independent" monopolies survive against competition and changes in our culture. It varies from nation to nation, but most of the long-term monopolies we experience are those regulated or run by the state, in such industries as mediums of exchange (money), medicine, utilities, roads, education, defense, power supply, communication, police, and the judicial system. Here we sometimes end up having to pay for a service whether it's efficient or not, whether we need it or not, and with little or no option to choose our supplier for that service.

Potentially, a government is the most dangerous threat to man's rights: it holds a legal monopoly on the use of physical force against legally disarmed victims.

Ayn Rand, Russian-American novelist, 1905–1982

There are exceptions to the above points and they are exceptions—not the rule. In an increasingly communications-rich world it becomes both difficult and unprofitable for a business of any size to disregard the morals and considerations of the society upon which it depends for that buck, whether fast or slow. And while I lament the way in which entire untainted populations will sometimes eagerly embrace the crasser aspects of Western culture, I do not complain about their right to do so. I am dismayed, however, when aspects of their own culture and tradition are banned or discouraged in response to global pressure for culture to fit the Western corporate consumerist model. Do it our way, or else!

Most valid examples of coercive abuse from the corporate world have either passed into history, or are carried out in collusion with a state. The former are historical because the resulting publicity and public disenchantment with direct coercive action by business is damaging to their image. When the public sees a banana producer or a car manufacturer's hirelings shooting strikers, they retaliate with their wallets. Many examples of corporate abuse persist today, where a corporation has enlisted the state to do the dirty work it could not do itself. Whether it is tribal farmers in Guatemala murdered to pursue World Bank-supported dam projects, or indigenous communities evicted when mineral rights to their ancient lands are sold to Western companies, it is the state with its soldiers and police who are there to do the dirty work, paid for by the purchase of "rights" from the state. Companies cannot easily get away with naked coercion in today's world. Hell, even the police are having a difficult time getting away with indiscriminate beating and killings, now likely to be broadcast worldwide within minutes. The fact that two men in a garage successfully challenged the all-powerful giant, IBM, speaks volumes about the vulnerability of a corporate Goliath to the power of unfettered creative competition.

We are all aware of the depths to which businesses (and people) will sink in the quest for wealth, and often have personal experience of lies, deceptions, and dishonoring of promises. When this has happened, when we finally recognize the deception of a business or colleague, whether in advertising or employment promises, we are in a position to stop buying the product or working with the person. However severe the disruption and inconvenience of doing this, we do not go to jail for our actions—our desire for freedom does not result in the loss of our freedom.

Can we really hope that the state, disconnected from the feedback loop of our society, is going to make big business safer and more ethical, when we regularly witness the state exceeding the corruption of corporations, while aiding and abetting their worst abuses? In the dangerous combination of big business and the state, it is the agency of the state that usually creates or officially condones the damage. Only we can protect ourselves from the dangers posed by the growth of big corporations, and the sooner we empower ourselves with this awareness the better. Because they cannot force the money from our pockets, we, their customers, have more ultimate control of their activities than do their own boardroom or the state. And in most matters of life we are able to exercise this control invisibly without the need to attend board meetings, consider too many issues, or tick from limited selections in different boxes.

Disclaimer: *Do not be swayed by the above propaganda. All businesses are run by evil twisted people who would sell their grandmother if the price were right. Everything on sale anywhere is a rip-off, and you should really be making all your own stuff, from pencils to bicycles, drugs to smartphones. Only then can you escape the evils of the free enterprise system.*

22

The Arms Industry Toilet

The arms industry is often cited as a productive component of our society, creating jobs, employment, and exports. As we shall see, this is a false assertion and weapons manufacture is more damaging than just about any other industry on the planet, including pharmaceuticals, sex trafficking, illegal drugs, and the oil and mining industries. It wastes precious resources, both human and material.

But first, is it any coincidence that the two most successful economic recoveries in the years after the Second World War were in the two countries forbidden to spend on arms or standing armies after their defeat? Can it be an accident that when you do not throw a large chunk of the nation's wealth down the toilet, the rest of the economy does a lot better? Perhaps this was key to making Japan and Germany, in 2012, the third and fourth largest economies in the world. Since the war, the victors (America, Russia, Britain, and France) have poured large sums into the arms industry and procured positions as suppliers of military hardware to the nations of the world. At the same time they maintain oversized standing armies and an inefficient, dangerous, and costly nuclear power establishment, built in order to support the production of nuclear weapons.

The fundamental difference between the arms industry and the majority of other commercial enterprises is that the value of military product is *negative*. This is an important concept. Large sums of society's money are spent manufacturing weapon products that we hope *never to use.* Assuming the weapons are not put to use, then considerable further sums are wasted looking after them, updating them, destroying old stocks, and maintaining a force of people ready and willing to use them if ever ordered to do so. And even though one country might seem to profit from selling these items to another, our global society as a whole is dragged down by the weight of their uselessness and literally torn apart if they are put to use. For if and when these products are used, an even greater cost becomes apparent. When weapon products are deployed, they tend to dramatically decrease the value of other products that we already possess, including our lives.

The contrast with productive products like the train or truck, the smartphone, and the sewing machine could not be greater, since these devices enable us to do useful things that add value to the lives of people and other products of planet Earth. We (you and me) don't buy the military technology, traded between and used by a very exclusive club, although the product itself is bought with money taken from our pockets in one country or another. Money we have justly earned with our energy and intellect, trucks and computers, is being flushed down a toilet that could easily take us with it.

Undoubtedly, while our world is run by a collection of coercively based states, we need to have what protection we can from the Hitlers, Bushes, Blairs, Pol Pots, and countless others who assume leadership of nations, and with it the power to do great damage. Of course, every bad guy's biggest dream is to take control of a nation, complete with a tax collecting base and population that is used to being under control. It might have taken centuries for this state structure to develop its power base, but it can take just a few months for a new and powerful despot to gain control. There will always be unsavory people seeking to manipulate or control any organization that has legitimized its right to take money from the population by force. The great challenge facing humanity is to one day arrive at a condition where there is no powerful state in this position of control.

> *A thousand years scarce serve to form a state. An hour may lay it in the dust.*
>
> Byron, 1788–1824, *Childe Harold's Pilgrimage*

Sadly, when governments collapse today, the popular mindset is always limited to keeping the same structure and putting new people with fresh ideas in charge. But it is the structure that is at fault, and if we allow our society to self-govern, as did my ancestral Dithmarscheners in the fifteenth and sixteenth centuries and the medieval cities of twelfth and thirteenth century Europe, we would for once experience real democracy (self-rule). In this state, we would be in a position to prevent future despots or fanatics starting from scratch and building coercive structures large enough to take anything over by force.

We have been told for decades by the world's great powers that their armaments buy us peace and a safe climate in which to develop our society. Yet from the examples that history has given us, it does not appear that a strong and successful arms industry and military establishment are signs of a healthy society—one able to endure and improve for future generations. Many of the world's great empires collapsed soon after reaching the peak of their military strength. Yet this "Who's got the biggest dick" attitude to arms acquisition is typical for the rulers of most large modern states.

The negative effect of arms industry and military expenditure is enormous when the full costs are recognized, and it is no surprise that they result in the collapse of communities and social disorder. Enormous sums are worse than wasted, instead of being productively re-circulated in the society that created the wealth. Most visible are the fixed military overhead of feet on the ground and facilities. Each year another trillion or so dollars are spent adding to their arsenals. Millions are employed in maintaining, storing, and guarding these deadly military "assets." Within the total cost we can include the wasted education and skills of those who devise new ways of killing us, and that of the engineers who turn these negative ideas into lethal weapons products. We must include the loss of many precious resources of the planet and the lost productive capacity of those producing the weaponry as well as those killed by it. And there are the widows, the disabled, the refugees, the orphans, and the famines caused by war. How do we put a value on those idyllic islands and other areas of our planet destroyed forever or rendered uninhabitable for millennia by war or weapons testing? Consider also the vast expanse of desert in Nevada where obsolete American warplanes are parked wing to wing as far as the eye can see, and the mountains in nearby New Mexico that have been hollowed to store obsolete nuclear warheads. Finally, we have the ongoing costs arising from the regular re-introduction into society of those who have been trained to kill their fellow human beings. How can a stable society continue to suffer this expense, which is extracted in order to bring us security from other countries that buy arms so that their society is secure from us? We need security, but with two World Wars in memory, dozens of major wars, ongoing conflicts across the world, and an endless amorphous war on terrorism, it is apparent that our traditional approach is tragically flawed.

Overgrown military establishments are under any form of government inauspicious to liberty, and are to be regarded as particularly hostile to republican liberty.

George Washington, first US President, 1732–1799

So don't buy the argument that the weapons industry creates employment, or that it is good for the economy, security, or peace. It would be better for our overall economy to take the vast amount of government money spent on arms purchases, pile it into an enormous heap, and set fire to it. Better yet, leave the money working in society in the first place. In order to do this, we will first need to find more innovative ways of preventing the Germans, French, Koreans, Chinese, Brazilians, or Libyans from taking over the Houses of Parliament and government of Great Britain or Washington DC. I doubt we need fear them taking over the offices of the European Commission in Brussels.

Peace will ultimately arise from cooperation, freedom, and an absence of the obsession with where borderlines are drawn on the map; not from our possession of more and more lethal and dangerous weaponry. What could be more obvious?

23

What's Wrong with Money?

Money and wealth are surrounded by so much emotion, envy, and aspiration that we can easily lose touch with what money actually is, or rather what it represents.

Volumes have been written and fortunes made on books telling us how to make loads of money and how to invest it once we've got it. We have multiple means of borrowing money and we know something about its history. As an avid young coin collector, I once thrilled to think of the lives my little slugs of metal had known so many centuries ago. These days, with bankers increasingly revealed to be banksters, we are awash with revelations of the confidence trick that has been played on us and the iniquity of those with the power to create money from thin air. We are coming face to face with the consequences of moving from value-based currencies to fiat currencies (paper money representing nothing) in 1971 when the gold standard was abandoned.

The concept of responsible banking is a useful one and it is tragic that the sector has come to control, milk, and manipulate the money supply, rather than manage and facilitate the flow of wealth that we create with our minds and our bodies and our clever tools. But lots of money can sometimes do weird things to people, especially when their hands are on the controls of whatever puppets appear to be running the country.

Though the money we now use is based on little of any substance, it remains a simple and useful way to represent the real value that we create when turning metal into cooking pots or inspiration into music. As well as precious metals, things ranging from cowry shells to jade, eggs to feathers, and salt to vodka have been used as money at one time and place or another. Money is a real and worthwhile concept, and if we didn't have it, we would need to invent it. We are re-inventing it now with Bitcoins and various forms of LETS (local exchange trading systems) in cities and regions across the world; there are over one hundred such schemes in Ecuador alone. This is social evolution taking place; we humans are great at this kind of stuff when the need is there and our actions are not governed by stifling legislation. These new systems are destined to grow and prosper as the fiat system falters.

When inspiration becomes a beautiful tune; a few pennies worth of clay a coffee mug; or silicon, metal, genius, and plastic a smartphone, a value has been added to the world. When knowledge and experience evolve as each generation shares what it knows with the next one, value is added to the world. The farmer creates value when converting sunlight, air, water, and Earth into rice and beans and eggs and cabbages. Something that was once worth a little bit less, or very little at all, has been changed into something more valuable through the application of human ingenuity, intellect, skill, and effort. We represent this value with money, and it is a major root source of our wealth as a society. The other source of value is natural resources such as oil, metal, minerals, salt, sand, and so forth, all requiring some human interface to become of value. This is the underlying value of money in this world, even if money creation itself originates from debt.

It is this value, or the capacity to produce it, that is traded as company shares in financial markets, for gain or loss. The basis of this wealth can be real, unlike many of the complex financial instruments that have so undermined Western economies. When wet clay is turned into a mug, wealth has been created and it has been at nobody's expense. I only make this elaborate point for those who suspect that money is inherently evil, or always made at the expense of somebody, somewhere else. That unfortunately happens too, but the value that shifts in many financial transactions had to be created in the first place.

What a shame it is that so many of those involved in valuable and important work on this planet do so with the attitude that they should not make any money or profit from their good works. Dedicated companies or individuals who come up with means to save the rainforest and the rhinoceros, house the homeless, and feed the hungry are doing valuable work. I wish them a healthy financial reward for their efforts and hope their example will inspire others to emulate their activity. Why not get stinking rich from saving the rainforest—from providing such immense value to planet Earth and humanity? Money is not the root of all evil, though "love of money" does underlie much of the evil out there, especially when combined with dubious moral standards and the power to pass and enforce laws.

Money is like love; it kills slowly and painfully the one who withholds it, and enlivens the other who turns it on his fellow man.

Kahlil Gibran, Lebanese-American writer, 1883–1931

The idea of money itself is fine despite the debased, false, and fragile version of it that we experience. Don't feel bad about your value being appreciated with money, but do not forget the very real value of just being appreciated and helping people out. This author enjoyed many of his early years introducing natural and organic foods to the UK, though ended up teetering on the verge of bankruptcy after fifteen years of it. When in 1982 I created, christened, and launched the original VegeBurger, it did well and for once in my life there was more money coming in than going out. It really felt good and I am unabashed about acknowledging that.

The reality and stability of money are sticky as hell. This upgrade is written in 2012 and the whole stack of cards looks in danger of collapsing if any one card goes. We see central banks and governments desperately mortgaging future generations to keep the rickety structure propped up. Greece may be deeper in the pit than Europe and the US, but the walls to be scaled appear unassailable at this stage to any of them. I'm no investment advisor or strategist and have never paid too much attention to money, but I do understand that all fiat currencies have ultimately collapsed, so to actually witness it happening and see what replaces it should at least be very interesting. We are human beings, able to find a way around problems and figure new ways to do things, as we have done throughout ancient and recent history. Bring it on!

24

Banking and Banksters

Presidents and pop stars, political parties and crime dynasties, corporations and cafes, empires and alliances all have one thing in common: over time, they come and they go. In the course of it, they keep us diverted by generating the constant stories of competition and conflict that fill our news and thoughts today, as well as most of our drama and entertainment. Bankers and banking do not belong in this grouping.

While we exercise our minds over politicians' excessive expense accounts, presidential sex habits, phony foreign wars, prominent pedophiles, and the trials and tribulations of the famous, our minds rarely stray to the far more obscure, boring, and hidden matters of international finance. The LIBOR banking scandal of 2012, involving trillions of dollars, makes Al Capone, Britain's Great Train Robbery, and Bonnie and Clyde's activities seem like petty crimes, but it is far too incomprehensible and boring for most and unlikely to ever be immortalized by a box office hit. The severity of bankers' moral transgressions is highlighted by fines from the hundreds of millions to over a billion dollars, yet none go to prison for their crimes, instead being effectively allowed to treat the fines as business operating costs. Unlike fines imposed for industrial accidents, oil spills, and drunk driving, the bankers' crimes are intentional, deceptive, and fraudulent. How can they avoid incarceration?

"Give me control of a nation's money supply, and I care not who makes its laws," declared Mayer Amschel Rothschild, founder of his family's banking dynasty in the eighteenth century. Once the money supply is in private bankers' hands, it becomes almost impossible to wrest it back without inflicting great hardship and turmoil on the populace. And once in these central bankers' hands, it becomes possible for money to literally be created out of thin air, quite legally. We can see why banking is such an attractive industry, paying lavish salaries and bonuses to those who are able to understand and work its machinations.

In the United Kingdom, which touts itself as the world's financial capital, every bank note carries a bizarre statement, signed by the Chief Cashier of the Bank of England. This is the solemn promise "to pay the bearer on demand the sum of XY pounds." Well, you already have that XY pounds in your hand, since it is no more than a piece of paper saying it is worth a piece of paper that says it is worth XY pounds. Cash in on their promise and they will just give you back another piece of paper saying the same thing. This is a useful promise if you have somehow spilled sardine oil on your banknotes, but otherwise it is useless. Things have changed from the days when Britain's Pound Sterling was exchangeable for a pound of sterling silver (454 grams).

This is the reason that "fiat" currency is so inherently flimsy. It is based on nothing, which makes it easy to steadily print more of it every year. Every extra bit that is printed directly reduces the value of the money already in circulation, inflating prices and stealing from the communal pocket. This is why, in the US and most of Europe, counterfeiting was considered a serious enough crime to carry the death penalty well into the nineteenth century; in the late twentieth century it effectively became government policy. When money was linked to something real, inflation was not an automatic feature of the money supply. The price of bread was lower in the eighteenth century than it had been in the sixteenth. In 1695 the average Briton spent £3.85 on food per annum. It hadn't changed much a century later, and then inflation began to creep into the picture, later compounded by packaging, convenience, and regulation.

We have historical accounts of rampant inflation arising as the Roman Empire gradually reduced the 95 percent silver denarius to nothing more than a copper coin dipped in tin. Though we came into the twentieth century with minimal inflation, it has been picking up since, boosted during wartime as bankers print money to lend governments to finance their fight, getting their payback in cash from the winner and hard assets from the loser. After the First World War, the German Weimar Republic began printing money to pay its bills, with over two hundred factories eventually working flat out to supply the banknotes. Rampant inflation soon followed, lifting the price of a loaf of bread from one mark in 1919 to one hundred billion marks in November 1923.

Since the mid-1950s inflation has been gaining momentum in most of the Western world, spurred on anew by QE (quantitative easing), the latest euphemism for printing money. The world's three major currencies, the dollar, pound, and euro, have all been at it. After several generations of living with inflation, we've almost come to see it as something traditional that is a normal part of the money system. Governments even talk about "target" inflation rates as if that is something healthy to achieve rather than just something not as bad as a higher number. It has no use or valid place in the money system. There is no underlying need for the cost of living to increase year upon year.

One of the great strengths of the banks is the impenetrable complexity of their operations. There is nothing complex, though, about how they literally create money out of thin air through the fractional reserve banking system. This legally permits banks to lend out money they don't have, based on how much they do have, which doesn't have to be much. This state-sanctioned activity arises from the fraudulent activity of early goldsmiths who took gold into safekeeping, giving people certificates of ownership of that gold. These certificates started to be traded as money and even though gold was sometimes withdrawn, on balance the goldsmith always had more or less stable stocks. At some point goldsmiths realized they could issue more tradable certificates than there was gold in storage, effectively creating money. This would only come to light if enough depositors decided to withdraw their gold at once, an unlikely occurrence. This fraudulent and inflationary practice became so inherent to banking that it was legalized once the bankers had their hands firmly gripping the genitals of the nation.

In simple terms, if a community of ten people all put $1,000 into the bank and the fractional reserve rate is set at 10 percent, the bank has the power to lend ten times that amount, $100,000, back to the public. Thus each of those depositors, offering his or her house or assets as security, could borrow $10,000 from the bank, or two of them might borrow $50,000. Thus, the bank sits on $10,000 in deposits from its depositors, and has $100,000 out as secured loans, which have now miraculously become interest-earning assets of the bank. If the borrower cannot repay the debt, then the bank takes on ownership of his or her house, car, or other security. The act of creating a debt to the bank by the borrower is the primary source of money creation in the current economic structure, and another stimulus to inflation. I have used 10 percent for easy mental calculation. At the time of writing a 10 percent rate applies only in Bulgaria and Mexico; reserves requirements vary from 1 percent in the Eurozone to 20 percent in China and Brazil. Furthermore, should some borrowers decide to deposit some of the money in another bank, then that bank can lend out ten times that sum, and so on.

Banking is a deeply confusing and opaque industry and I make no apology for not attempting to make clear to the reader exactly how banks do what they do, or how they get away with it. As relevant as it is, it is also deeply uninteresting and I repeat myself in saying that this is one of the banking industry's greatest strengths. The charge has often been leveled that the shadowy dynasties running the world's central banks are also major shapers of laws and policies that ensure no threat arises to their rule; that they consciously plan economic booms and busts in order to reap great harvests from the general misfortune thus inflicted; that they often finance both sides in the world's major wars and conflicts, ensuring their success regardless of who wins; or that the money they create is invested in hard inflation-proof areas such as minerals, natural resources, agribusiness, power generation, and so on.

Few of us will understand how a situation arose during the early twenty-first century whereby the taxpayer ended up bailing out banks with hundreds of billions of dollars, pounds, and euros. It is the central banks of Europe, the UK, and the US that will electronically generate that bailout money and credit it to commercial banks, leaving the state in debt to the central bank for that money. The state has to recoup this handout from us, leaving the debt on the shoulders of today's taxpayers and their descendants. Our futures have been sold to the banks as tax-generating assets, and an ever-increasing percentage of overall taxation will be applied to servicing government debt to the bankers.

Am I being simplistic? Perhaps. As I said, banking is a confusing and impenetrable business. However, those who have had intimate experience of banking, from inside and outside the industry, are quite clear about what lies behind the smoke and mirrors. Historic warnings abound about letting banks control the money supply but, alas, there is little advice on what to do once they have control. I will let some of these characters close this chapter, should you not be sufficiently convinced by my words alone.

What do bankers, statesmen, and Henry Ford have to say about banking?

> *Give me control of a nation's money supply, and I care not who makes its laws.*

Mayer Amschel Rothschild, founder of the dynasty,
1744–1812

> *The bank hath benefit of interest on all moneys which it creates out of nothing.*

William Paterson, founder in 1694 of the Bank of England,
a privately owned bank until 1946, which in 1977 yielded
most of its power back to the private sector

> *I sincerely believe that banking establishments are more dangerous than standing armies; and that the principle of spending money to be paid by posterity, under the name of funding, is but swindling futurity on a large scale.*

Thomas Jefferson, American Founding Father, 1743–1826

History records that the money changers have used every form of abuse, intrigue, deceit, and violent means possible to maintain their control over governments by controlling money and its issuance.

James Madison, US President, 1751–1836

I care not what puppet is placed on the throne of England to rule the Empire. The man who controls Britain's money supply controls the British Empire and I control the British money supply.

Nathan Rothschild, 1777–1836

Banks lend by creating credit. They create the means of payment out of nothing.

Sir Ralph George Hawtrey, economist and distinguished professor, 1879–1975

If the American people ever allow private banks to control the issue of their money, first by inflation and then by deflation, the banks and corporations that will grow up around them, will deprive the people of their property until their children will wake up homeless on the continent their fathers conquered.

Thomas Jefferson, American Founding Father, 1743–1826

I fear that foreign bankers with their craftiness and tortuous tricks will entirely control the exuberant riches of America and use it to systematically corrupt civilization.

Otto von Bismarck, German Chancellor, after the assassination of Abraham Lincoln

It is well enough that people of the nation do not understand our banking and money system, for if they did, I believe there would be a revolution before tomorrow morning.

Henry Ford, founder of the Ford Motor Company,
1863–1947

The real truth of the matter is, as you and I know, that a financial element in the large centers has owned the government ever since the days of Andrew Jackson.

Franklin D. Roosevelt, in a letter to Colonel House in 1933

The responsibility for the last World War [WW I] rests solely upon the shoulders of the international financiers. It is upon them that rests the blood of millions of dead and millions of dying.

1924 Congressional Record, 67th Congress

. . . Our whole monetary system is dishonest, as it is debt-based . . . We did not vote for it. It grew upon us gradually but markedly since 1971 when the commodity-based system was abandoned.

The Earl of Caithness, in a speech to the
House of Lords, 1997

I am afraid the ordinary citizen will not like to be told that the banks can and do create money. And they who control the credit of the nation direct the policy of Governments and hold in the hollow of their hand the destiny of the people.

Reginald McKenna, Chairman of the Midland Bank, to
stockholders in 1924

The few who understand the system will either be so interested in its profits or be so dependent upon its favors that there will be no opposition from that class, while on the other hand, the great body of people, mentally incapable of comprehending the tremendous advantage that capital derives from the system, will bear its burdens without complaint, and perhaps without even suspecting that the system is inimical to their interests.

The Rothschild brothers of London, writing to associates in New York, 1863

The study of money, above all other fields in economics, is one in which complexity is used to disguise truth or to evade truth, not to reveal it. The process by which banks create money is so simple the mind is repelled. With something so important, a deeper mystery seems only decent.

John Kenneth Galbraith, former professor of economics at Harvard, 1908–2006

The drive of the Rockefellers and their allies is to create a one-world government combining super capitalism and Communism under the same tent, all under their control . . . Do I mean conspiracy? Yes I do. I am convinced there is such a plot, international in scope, generations old in planning, and incredibly evil in intent.

US Congressman Larry P. McDonald, 1976

Some even believe we (the Rockefeller family) are part of a secret cabal working against the best interests of the United States, characterizing my family and me as "internationalists" and of conspiring with others around the world to build a more integrated global political and economic structure—one world, if you will. If that's the charge, I stand guilty, and I am proud of it.

David Rockefeller, 1915–

25

Strange Fruit

It was Britain's Margaret Thatcher who popularized the concept of combining the coercive power of the state with the creativity and efficiency of our free enterprise culture. There was, perhaps, some glimmer of sense in the concept itself. Unfortunately, by introducing the coercive "Do it or we'll damage you" formula into the equation, the state severs the feedback loop that enables things to work without the need for anybody to be cracking a whip.

At its most benign this combination just results in us paying the state to select whom we pay to do the job, as is the case with contracting out waste collection services to private companies rather than using council employees and council-owned vehicles. It also establishes the rationale and mechanism to charge us for services once covered by local government taxes, as has happened in the UK where, for instance, charges are often levied to park in front of one's own house.

But the results of this combination often bear strange fruit, and the very strangest of these indeed must be the wheel clamp. In the UK, "private enterprise" firms are engaged by local councils to seek out and punish vehicle owners who have parked where the state has decided they should not park. These are, one might reasonably assume, places where a parked car is likely to inconvenience or endanger pedestrians or other road users. When these firms find someone so parked, or find a parking meter tenant who has overstayed the allotted period, they call in the clamping van, which will then often double-park alongside the offending vehicle. Aware that they are creating further road blockage, the highly trained team jumps out and within moments are away again, having attached a large yellow immobilizing clamp onto a wheel of the car. When the driver returns, the process required to remove the clamp takes from thirty minutes to two hours or more and costs well over £100.

It would seem obvious that this punishment for the transgression serves only to prolong the offense that has been committed, increasing the danger that is meant to be prevented. Imagine using this technique in other areas of human endeavor. You are four days late in paying the monthly rent on your apartment. As retribution the landlord locks you into your apartment for two months and demands six months' rent before he will let you out. Perhaps it could be applied to drunken drivers who are forced as punishment to drink a very expensive bottle of whisky and then drive home. If there is a reason not to park somewhere, then it defies common sense to punish the offender by exacerbating the offense. Yet when the coercive state is involved, common sense is not, and combining this with private enterprise is a dangerous approach indeed.

The madness of wheel clamping may be diminishing in the UK, replaced by private companies operating many thousands of both fixed and car-mounted cameras feeding computers that dispatch whopping fines through the old-fashioned post every time they snap you being naughty. Less labor costs. The victim may have just dropped somebody off, or strayed into a cycle lane at 4 AM when there was no other traffic on the roads. Private firms are also busy handing out fines to those who overstay their time at a parking meter. An extra £1 may have bought enough time for the parker to return twenty minutes later, avoiding a fine of £120 for doing no more than failing the foresight test by five minutes. It makes no sense until we acknowledge that such behavior genuinely merits the term "highway robbery."

Now we are seeing local governments rely increasingly on fines against their constituents, and confiscation of assets, to supply a basic and budgeted portion of their income. When drivers get wise and budgets are not being met, new restrictions can be implemented to create more offenders. And none of this growing state income source is included when total taxation levels are calculated. Now that it is the fashion for governments to embrace the techniques of the free market, will we be seeing bold marketing initiatives coming from the traffic management departments of local councils? Why not give motorists the chance to buy five speeding fines or parking tickets in advance and get one free, for instance? And how about a jolly 25 percent Christmas discount on December wheel clamp removals and towaways? Rather than suspending the driving licenses of their best earners, the state should offer them a cashback bonus when their fines reach £1000 in a month, year, or whatever.

There are few mechanisms in the tool bag of the state to naturally encourage less wasteful lifestyles through opt-outs or incentives rather than punishment. Imagine that you could develop a comfortable lifestyle, recycling almost everything, producing a bare minimum of waste requiring removal. This would be great news for the planet and your community, yet there is no direct benefit to be had through less cost for your waste removal—just the good feeling that you are in a harmonious interface with the planet, which is enough to motivate some but not the many.

One of the most frightening strange fruits to come from the mating of coercion with free enterprise is the increased reliance on privatization of the prison industry. Here we have the state creating a private industry that relies upon the state's coercive power to supply it with a stream of new customers (inmates). This industry has become a strong lobby in support of maintaining and increasing those laws carrying prison sentences. As the Correctional Corporation of America warned in its 2010 annual report: "Any changes [in the laws] with respect to drugs and controlled substances or illegal immigration could affect the number of persons arrested, convicted and sentenced, thereby potentially reducing demand for correctional facilities to house them."

Private prisons have enjoyed many years as a "hot" investment stock in America since their introduction in the 1980s. In the three decades that followed we saw the American prison population increase five-fold, from one-half million to two and one-half million, during a time in which crimes, with or without victims, have remained relatively constant.

Just about every year, Congress passes another crime bill—spending billions of dollars to build more prisons, to place more Band-Aids on society's scars.

Carrie P. Meek, American congresswoman, 1926–

The coercive "Do it or I'll inflict damage upon you" approach has never been a successful long-term strategy for businesses, corporations, or small enterprises. Attempting to harness this approach with enterprise culture in order to make the state more efficient is accompanied by grave dangers with only an occasional cost-saving benefit.

26

Meat of the Issue

I think it could be plausibly argued that changes of diet are more important than changes of dynasty or even of religion.

George Orwell, *The Road to Wigan Pier*, 1937

We are used to hearing about the downside of meat consumption and the ethical questions raised by the degrading nature of its production. As originator of the Vege-Burger, I empathize with these views, but from a very different viewpoint. It has seemed to me for some time that perhaps we are doing domesticated animals a favor by including them in our food chain. I just don't think we *should* do them this favor, because the price we have to pay is too high. And I doubt the issue would be a problem were the state not so intricately involved at the primary end of our food chain, having for decades placed meat production on a pedestal above other agricultural practices. The interface that has developed with domesticated animals in the Western world bears all the hallmarks of a classic host-parasite relationship.

In this relationship it is quite plausible to view man as the host and domesticated animals as the parasites. Though we need not envy the lifestyle of the average chicken or cow, they have, together with sheep and pigs, done extraordinarily well on the evolutionary ladder as species. They have multiplied and flourished. In us, they have a host who diligently covers over 70 percent of our arable land in crops designed *not* to be eaten by humans, but to be fed to agricultural animals. While we are unable to adequately house our own species, vast acres of the country are covered in buildings built for the sole benefit of domesticated animals, who must ultimately pay the rent with their lives. The UN Environment Program reveals that 80 percent of the world's chemical fertilizers are applied to crops and pastures devoted to meat production. Over half of these fertilizers end up being washed into rivers and oceans, creating dead zones in the waters, and adding to acid rain and climate change.

What do we get in return, other than worldwide malnutrition and starvation due to this huge parasitic bite out of the food chain? Disease and food poisoning are the simple answer. The excessive consumption of animal products, made possible by state subsidies and the factory farm, has now been implicated in virtually every major degenerative disease of the West, and is the source of over 90 percent of food poisoning cases. Meanwhile, we have lost the efficiency of important antibiotics, as their routine inclusion in animal feed allows pathogens to develop immunity. Some are added purely as a growth stimulant and others to damp down infectious diseases in overcrowded factory farm conditions. The powerful agribusiness lobby has blocked all attempts by alarmed and concerned groups to limit agricultural use of antibiotics, stymying both the medical profession and government health departments.

As if the antibiotic drugs are not enough, many meat-producing nations continue to include hormones in animal feeds, to encourage rapid growth of body mass and muscle. These hormones might well prompt similar reactions in other mammals sharing from 80 to 95 percent of their DNA, such as human beings. We use hormones from pigs to provide insulin for human use, and hormones from horses for the HRT prescribed to some post-menopausal women. Would it be surprising to find that the various hormones added to animal feed are contributing to the rising obesity epidemic, and to an increasing incidence of breasts on men and facial hair on women?

During my years in the natural food business, I became aware of substantial subsidies that enabled producers of animal feed to buy cereals at prices much cheaper than those paid by flour millers or makers of breakfast cereal for human consumption. The wheat was "denatured" with blue dye to make sure nobody used it for human food. Do you know anyone who ever marched or lobbied under the "Cheap Food for Cows" banner? Yet we pay dearly with both our wallets and our health, as a result of the state's intervention and control of the food chain.

My personal belief is that the food we eat has a major impact on not only our physical health, but also our state of mind, our happiness, our fear, our peace, our anxiety. High consumption of dead animals who lived miserable lives and suffered horrific deaths helps feed the negative states of mind. But we have included flesh in our diet throughout our evolution, though rarely with the shameful disrespect for life exhibited by the factory farm. As omnivores, we are able to choose what we eat and can easily exclude the flesh of other animals, choosing our foods only from the vegetable world. I took this course from the age of ten to my mid-twenties, and completed my schooling without ever encountering another classmate who did not eat meat. Times have certainly changed!

Overconsumption of meat is the primary factor inhibiting this planet's ability to feed all of its inhabitants on sustainably farmed land. Livestock's methane emissions are a major contributor to greenhouse gases, and huge quantities of water are required, with effluent from the animals polluting our rivers and oceans. Humanity needs to respond, urgently. In Europe and the US, cultural leaders of the world, there has been a substantial increase in numbers of vegetarians and those reducing meat consumption. But this is not happening in China or Africa or South America. We cannot expect government to change anything by using their powers to ban some types of meat and prohibitively tax others—all in our interest, of course. It would be preferable to see a slow drift away from meat consumption as a shift in social behavior over twenty to one hundred years than have those running the state proclaim bans and create new squadrons of police to enforce them. Their numbers and powers would only grow as more and more abuse took place, pet disappearances needed investigation, and clandestine restaurants needed busting— all accompanied by further erosion of human rights.

A man can live and be healthy without killing animals for food; therefore, if he eats meat, he participates in taking animal life merely for the sake of his appetite.

Leo Tolstoy, Russian author, 1828–1910

I am not questioning whether it is moral or immoral to raise animals to kill and eat. I am simply pointing out that we are being taken for a ride and that it is foolhardy in the extreme to destroy the wide variety of natural flora and fauna of the countryside in order to support a handful of intensively farmed crops that are then fed to a handful of animal species to produce subsidized meat at the expense of the quality and price of our primary food sources. Our return on this misguided investment in meat consumption is anywhere from a quarter to a tenth of the nutrients that are put into producing the meat—and the resultant food that we eat is secondhand.

Perhaps there is a defensible argument to be made for rearing animals on the naturally occurring food waste of ingredients (like indigestible cereal husks and vegetable trimmings); for feeding them our domestic and catering throwaway; or for putting them out to graze in areas where arable food farming is not feasible. These animals would not have experienced the pleasure of life were they not part of the human food agenda (the same is true of apple trees, barley, and cabbages). Humane techniques of slaughter have been developed that prevent any stress from building up before the moment of stunning and death, and most organic farmers treat their animals well.

Future generations may, of course, look back at mammal farming for meat with the same horror that accompanies our look back at the practices of our slave-owning ancestors. They will wonder how anybody could point out that the slaughter was humane.

If God did not intend for us to eat animals, then why did he make them out of meat?

John Cleese, British actor, comedian, writer, 1939–

Without the range of subsidies that come straight from our (vegetarian and carnivorous) pockets anyway, the price of animal products and meat would rise to a price reflecting the real cost of production, substantially increasing the price. Meat consumption would reduce to the level of an occasional foodstuff rather than being the mainstay of many diets. That primary position was attained but a few generations ago due to state support, does not prevail in most of the world today, and never can without the accompaniment of widespread hunger, as other mammals feed at our own primary food source. This is further aggravated by today's strange practice of growing food for cars rather than people, with biofuel production now taking up millions of hectares worldwide and consuming 40 percent of the North American corn harvest. How can anyone have the nerve to suggest that there is not enough land to feed the planet sustainably when they can still find the space to grow food for automobiles?

Without the central interference by the European Union in its food chain, the UK would never have produced the vast surplus of unwanted beef that EU bureaucrats decided to feed back to the vegetarian cattle from which it came. This is how those clever people in Brussels temporarily reduced the notorious "mountain" of frozen beef they had bought to maintain guaranteed prices. Never in a free market situation could the laws of economics be so twisted that an industry feeds its finished product back to itself as a raw ingredient. It is like going to all the trouble of making a new road-ready, crash-tested automobile, knowing that you will promptly scrap it to use the recovered junk metal as the raw ingredient of your next production.

Today's continuing drift away from dedicated red meat consumption and towards more vegetable foods in the diet is accompanied by a growing appreciation of the mental and physical health benefits to be achieved thereby. Yet despite our shifting diet we are still being charged to support the damaging rape of our countryside in order to keep the natural feedback loops from filtering through to the marketplace as higher meat prices and reduced demand.

And don't be misled by the foolish question of "What do we do with all the animals if people stop eating them?" We put them back in their natural place in the food chain for those who wish to indulge in pre-eaten food, and stop putting them up in cheap hotels while feeding them mass-produced junk food. By relieving the pressure to devote every acre to agriculture, we enable the land to enrich itself rather than decline, making space for the variety of wild animals and birds that once shared this land with us. Foxes, falcons, and wood pigeons have become a common sight in London. Surely it is a sad state of affairs when the wild animals of the country begin moving into the city because the countryside has become hostile and alien to them.

Simply let the meat industry be a free part of the real world of material costs, supply, demand, and product liability to which every other business must attune itself. Meat would then be dethroned from its improper place at the top of our

food chain and restored to the quality and safety that pre-
vailed for most of our occasionally meat-eating ancestors.

> *The butcher does not relent at the bleating of the lamb;*
> *neither is the heart of the cruel moved with distress. But*
> *the tears of the compassionate are sweeter than dew-*
> *drops, falling from roses on the bosom of spring.*
>
> Akhenaton, Pharaoh who worshiped light and banned ani-
> mal sacrifice, 1380–1334 BCE

27

The Drugs Problem

The Drug War is fueled by the fact that at this historic moment . . . our politicians are suffering from enemy deprivation. Faced with the real problems of urban decay, slipping global competitiveness, and a deteriorating educational system, the government has decided instead to turn its energies toward the sixty million Americans who use illegal psychoactive drugs.

Timothy Leary, advocate of psychedelics, 1920–1996

The primary problem with drugs is that they are illegal and/or state-controlled. This counter-evolutionary state control of substances that we ingest for other than nutritional purposes is the root cause of virtually all the problems that people are concerned about in connection with drugs, drug abuse, and drug-related crime. Sure, all drugs have potential problems if abused. But we are human beings and we are able to make judgments about these things, and treat them with respect and caution—just as we must when we drive vehicles, have sex, or buy food from street vendors. Cannabis, magic mushrooms, peyote, opium, coca leaf extracts, and alcohol were all legal at the end of the nineteenth century, when only alcohol was regarded as a major social problem. A century later, we find that alcohol is the only consciousness-altering drug that remains legal, and it remains a major social problem.

It should not surprise us that young people, especially, seek to experiment with drugs that alter or enhance their perception of life, and that youths and adults seek a drug-granted respite from the predictability of everyday life. There's a menu full of options out there to choose from, but all of our choices are channeled towards alcohol. The biggest cause of alcoholism is, perhaps, the difficulty in obtaining safer, non-addictive, and less befuddling alternatives, cannabis in particular. During the 1990s alcohol consumption plummeted amongst Europe's youth, together with football hooliganism, as a wider selection of drugs became available, "ecstasy" in particular. Clubs and bars were losing a significant slice of their income to this competitor that made people feel great for less, and happy to drink water. Once they realized what was going on, the brewers mounted a skilled and successful campaign. Kids are once again drinking large amounts of alcohol, and the most likely white powder they will ingest is cocaine, which tends to encourage more drinking, not less.

It seems a reasonable desire for people to find some means to get "out of their heads" from time to time—to take a totally different perspective on life. Perhaps some new perspectives are needed in the world today, and the attraction to drugs is evolution trying to happen. We should be pleased that many of today's generation are avoiding the trap of alcohol addiction, together with the anti-social behavior, depression, trivia worship, and middle-age burnout that abusers risk. When not abused, alcohol can be an enjoyable and stimulating drug that is beneficial to our health and well-being. Alcohol has a well-earned place in our culture, but that place does not deserve to be defended by state legislation and turned into a drug monopoly.

Drugs are an integral part of our culture and, as we learned in school, they made up the core of the early international business that brought the world's differing cultures into trade with each other. Those products of trade included tobacco, alcohol, opium, tea, coffee, chocolate, cocaine, and sugar. Tea was such a costly drug in the pre-revolutionary US that users would season and eat the dried leaves after drinking the strong tea. Prior to the discovery of sugar cane, the sweetening for Europe had been expensive honey; the intense sugar hit was once a luxury drug. Today, we are made addicts from childhood, with many seeing it as a child's inalienable right to consume large quantities of sugary things. Yet it is clear that the effects of sugar consumption are more damaging than many illegal drugs, and that for many, sugar is a harder drug to kick. The other major items of trade were pepper and spices, products we might view as virtual drugs to the taste buds of the bland European palate of the mid-millennium. The glorious history of trade in the civilized world was firmly anchored in humanity's desire for new and diverse drugs and sensory inputs.

Under the pressure of the cares and sorrows of our mortal condition, men have at all times, and in all countries, called in some physical aid to their moral consolations—wine, beer, opium, brandy, or tobacco.

Edmund Burke, Irish statesman, author, orator, political theorist, and philosopher, 1729–1797

People have always sought to include drugs in their life-style for many non-medical reasons: whether to stay awake longer or to fall asleep sooner; whether to drown their sorrows or to better understand them; whether to enjoy a banter in the bar with friends or have mystic communication with a tree; whether to explore their dark side or say hello to the god within. Some drugs are not an escape from "reality" but a gateway to exploring the very nature of reality. Even the humble drug tea was first discovered by Buddhist monks, who used its stimulatory qualities in their quest for higher consciousness when meditating through the night. One could imagine how dismayed they would be at the level of tea abuse taking place in modern Britain.

Some of the banned drugs are not only less dangerous than alcohol—they are hardly dangerous at all, and can lead to behavior that is positive and beneficial for the individual and society. Such minimal risk is involved in using psilocybin mushrooms and cannabis that it is difficult to find figures relating to deaths, if any, arising from their usage. Ecstasy (E, MDMA, Molly) is responsible for fewer deaths each year than paracetamol, lightning hits, or beef consumption. And millions of happy users continue to use these drugs with far less damage than that experienced by alcohol drinkers, amphetamine abusers, cocaine sniffers, cigarette puffers, or chocolates gobblers. Adults, as they long have, should certainly discourage drug experimentation in children. All drugs carry some risk if abused, even aspirin and cough syrup. But if we wish to enjoy the benefits, then we have to accept the responsibility, just as we take care when we travel in our car or on our bike, or go horseback riding, skiing, or swimming in the ocean. Much of our life consists of balancing the risks in life with the benefits to be had.

Getting happy, loving, insightful, bursting with positive energy, able to dance all night, or just chilled out are all definitely nice things to do; on what basis is it claimed that these valuable experiences are invalid when a drug assists us in easily reaching the desired state of mind? Let the critics keep drinking their instant coffee, downloading instant music, and flying across the world in hours instead of weeks. Let them eat their microwaved dinners, sliced pre-baked bread and take-away fast food, working on processors performing billions of calculations per second. Let them connect instantly with anybody in the world and escape from reality on TV, smart-phone, or iPad. But are we allowed to access happiness, peace, vision, boundless energy, or deep feelings of love quickly and without great expense? Oh no, this must be done the long way, through years of training and abstinence; or purchased, if we are to believe the advertising, when you select the right brand of automobile, sanitary towel, or soft drink.

Contrast the state's complacency regarding what we put into our bodies under the guise of food with its concern over what we ingest to feed our heads (an apt phrase from the Sixties). With food, that basic and essential necessity of life, we can eat whatever we like for any reason whenever we want to. We are allowed to consume chemical food additives that have no natural equivalent on planet Earth. The state even assures us that all this stuff is safe, as they did with every now-banned food additive when it was still legal.

We are allowed to eat genetically modified foodstuffs, the likes of which could only have evolved in nature had you per-suaded and enabled a scorpion to mate with a tomato. We can freely consume four times as much food as we need, and more than our body can safely process. We can go on doing this as long as we please, consuming hamburgers, candy bars, and soft drinks all the way to our state-provided hospital death-bed if we so choose. In the early 1990s the American Surgeon General attributed 80 percent of all illness-related deaths to diet-related causes. Yet nobody will jail you anywhere in the world for eating yourself to death.

So who is protecting whom from what? We are being denied sovereignty of our own mind! How can the state have the effrontery to control and legislate what we do with our own state of mind? Just what is going on here? Literally, you can end up behind bars for puffing on a plant that makes you feel happy and loving, gives you no crunching hangover, and is safer than crossing the road or visiting a friend in hospital. Must some twenty-nine million Europeans and thirty-two million Americans continue to be branded as criminals for making this choice?

Cannabis is the most risk-free illegal drug in existence, with a recognized safe history going back thousands of years. It is a happier and safer alternative to alcohol that doesn't tend to the dangerous combination of diminished abilities and boundless self-confidence.

Since the precursor to this book, costlier super strong "skunk" strains have appeared on the market. These require greater caution, make cannabis easier to abuse, and have triggered psychotic reactions in a minority of younger smokers. Many smokers make a point of seeking out milder versions, while many growers still go for the highest return in an illegal market. The World Drug Report from 2011 reports that this adverse reaction arises from strains with a high THC content and a low level of cannabis' other active ingredient, cannabidiol, which has been shown to have anti-psychotic properties. It is a problem that can be corrected by conscientious growers and breeders, and one that does not exist for users of hashish and more traditional varieties of the plant's resinous buds.

There appears to be no statistical evidence linking cannabis consumption with actual dangerous driving. August 2003 UK House of Commons Research paper on cannabis says that "the impairment in driving skills does not appear to be severe, even immediately after taking cannabis, when subjects are tested in a driving simulator. This may be because people intoxicated by cannabis appear to compensate for their impairment by taking fewer risks and driving more slowly, whereas alcohol tends to encourage people to take greater risks and drive more aggressively." More recently a US-based auto insurer (*4autoinsurancequote.org*) published a study showing that cannabis smokers were, statistically speaking, safer drivers than non-smokers. The US National Highway Transportation Safety Administration said that driving under the influence of marijuana "might even make you a safer driver," and found that cannabis users have accident responsibility rates below that of drug-free drivers. Yet penalties remain harsh for any driver testing positive on cannabis, for no sensible reason.

Cannabis is a drug, and use can turn to abuse and lead to reduced focus and motivation; this is a risk that is easier for a pot user to deal with when it occurs than it is for an alcohol user. And when it does occur, it is usually when cannabis is taken in combination with the addictive drug tobacco. Together they become a new drug that is pleasurable but addictive and tending more to abuse as a result. You are more likely to hear pure smokers talk about getting high and tobacco mixers about getting stoned.

> *Marijuana, in its natural form, is one of the safest therapeutically active substances known to man . . . It would be unreasonable, arbitrary and capricious for DEA to continue to stand between those sufferers and the benefits of this substance in light of the evidence in this record.*
>
> Findings of Senior US DEA Administrative Law
> Judge Francis Young, 1986

There are no confirmed published cases worldwide of human deaths from cannabis poisoning.

The Lancet, November 18, 1998

By comparison, tobacco is attributed to some 450,000 deaths each year in the US. Alcohol, which is directly responsible for over 85,000 US deaths each year, is also as a major contributor to the incidence of murder, violent crime, rape, suicide, fire, and drowning.

Make the most of the Indian hemp seed, and sow it everywhere!

George Washington's note to gardener at
Mount Vernon, 1794

Cannabis smoking was never perceived as a major threat to society, or associated with crime, until the 1930s, when the fanatical and ambitious Harry J. Anslinger became America's first drug czar. He made it his major mission to eradicate smoking of the "evil" drug marijuana, thereby undermining cultivation of the hemp plant on which it flowers. He had the backing and support of publishing baron William Randolph Hearst and his timber-owning buddies, in whose interest it was to wipe out hemp cultivation. It was the threat of hemp's competition against timber as the raw material for paper that motivated the press magnate to give considerable media backing to Anslinger. America's thousands of hemp farmers would soon have to change crops or go bust.

Marijuana is taken by ... musicians. And I'm not speaking about good musicians, but the jazz type ...

Harry J. Anslinger, Federal Bureau of Narcotics, 1948

The cannabis plant, hemp, can produce up to four times as much paper per acre as trees, and was the world's main agricultural crop for three thousand years. It was the first US agricultural product ever referred to as a "billion dollar" crop—in a 1938 *Popular Mechanics* article, which read: " . . . a machine has been invented which solves a problem more than 6,000 years old. The machine is designed for removing the fiber-bearing cortex from the rest of the stalk, making hemp fiber available for use without a prohibitive amount of human labor. Hemp is the standard fiber of the world . . . and can be used to produce more than 25,000 products ranging from dynamite to cellophane." Getting "high" is just a minor fringe benefit that this wonderfully useful plant offers our culture.

Drug czar Harry Anslinger and a couple curious "specialists" heavily promoted the movie *Reefer Madness*, a bizarre piece of anti-cannabis propaganda made in 1936. My father graphically remembers being shown it at age fourteen, when it was being screened to teachers and students throughout the US. Its hysterical attitude, epitomized by a man going crazy and stabbing his girlfriend to death after a frenzied few puffs on a joint, defined America's paranoid attitude to pot smoking for many years to come. Those who profit from pot's continued illegality use more sophisticated techniques today, and are still winning the propaganda war despite the fact that nearly all of the official reports commissioned by governments, here and abroad, have come out in favor of legalization.

> *It really puzzles me to see marijuana connected with narcotics, dope, and all of that stuff. It is a thousand times better than whiskey. It is an assistant and a friend.*
>
> Louis Armstrong, 1901–1971

The class of drugs referred to as psychedelics have their original roots and inspiration in natural substances that have for millennia been our tools as we explore altered states of consciousness, seeking a deeper understanding of life and the mysteries of the Universe. The state bans these substances for the same reason that it issues passports and control which borderlines we cross. They take us to territory the state would rather we left undiscovered and unexplored. Psychedelics are the traveling drugs—they do not, generally speaking, work by stimulating or reducing urges or inhibitions. They are not addictive, and have the fewest fatalities associated with them of virtually any class of drug.

> *I have no words to explain the effect the LSD had on me, although, I can say it was a positive life-changing experience for me and I am glad I went through that experience . . . one of the two or three most important things in [my] life.*
>
> Steve Jobs, 1955–2011

They give us a new perspective on our familiar world, as we travel to other dimensions and connect with the spirit that accompanies the physical world. In many ways the familiar world we live in, with houses, plumbers, parliaments, smart-phones, cars, roads, wars, button-up shirts, bread, and so forth is but one channel on the set of all possible channels. Since this is the "reality" we have created within the world around us, we are tuned to it to such a degree that we can easily become oblivious to the deeper nature of the vast Universe that encompasses the little fleck of matter in space that we call Earth.

Psychedelics are not taken as an "escape" from this world but as a ticket to see it from a different perspective, perhaps from a different dimension. It is hard to emerge from this voyage without developing a realization, amongst many others, that those "in power" are possessed of a narrow vision fueled primarily by the desire to stay in power. Their viewpoint is of one channel only—the one that represents the status quo in whatever country they control—and their efforts to fine-tune this channel to a micro degree can often appear ludicrous. Thus, these drugs reveal clearly that "the emperor has no clothes" and therefore must be prohibited at all costs.

> *I'm glad mushrooms are against the law, because I took them one time, and you know what happened to me? I laid in a field of green grass for four hours going, "My God! I love everything." Yeah, now if that isn't a hazard to our country . . . how are we gonna justify arms dealing when we realize that we're all one?*
>
> Bill Hicks, American comedian and satirist, 1961–1994

Many of the psychedelics grow naturally and have been utilized from the early days of our species along with the many other gifts of the Earth that we use to feed, clothe, and heal ourselves. LSD had its origins in the work of Dr. Albert Hoffman, who had a hunch that rye fungus ergot might yield some interesting drugs to his employers, Swiss drug firm Sandoz. First synthesized in the same year as the atom bomb, LSD exploded into the popular consciousness and kick-started the Sixties before it was banned. People never "looked within" before that—there was nothing there but intestines, muscles, organs, and stuff.

In the 1970s, chemist and psychonaut Alexander Shulgin, referred to as the stepfather of ecstasy, began experimenting with the MDMA molecule that created such a pleasurable sensation, and discovered over two hundred other psychoactive substances, most of which have now been banned. The latest new passports to enter our culture and attract persecution are the sacred plant medicines used since antiquity by indigenous peoples. Ayahuasca, peyote, and other ancient traveling tools are being increasingly explored in the West, with a sense of respect and usually with an experienced shaman in attendance. Many profess to feeling transformed and reborn by the experience of trying them.

Unlike our experiences with tobacco, alcohol, cocaine, chocolate, or heroin, we do not encounter users of psychedelics who continue to take these drugs while professing a constant desire to quit taking them. Many profess to experiencing profound healing with psychedelics—on physical, emotional, and spiritual levels—but if the experience is neither enjoyed nor beneficial, then there is never an urge to repeat it. They are powerful and dose-sensitive drugs, and in a legal climate buyers could be assured of dose and purity, reducing to zero the risk of accidentally taking too much and having an unpleasant time. Psychedelics should always be treated with respect, and are capable of giving stern reminders when this is not done. It is rare, too, for smokers of pure marijuana (tobacco-free) to continue smoking while professing their desire to stop.

Not all drugs are as safe and non-addictive as cannabis. Some, like heroin, cocaine, and controlled pharmaceuticals, carry serious risks and can create dependency and addiction. These are routinely made illegal in the belief that this will reduce consumption. The evidence could not be more to the contrary. Both the organized drug dealers and police forces grow in strength and stand to make more money or preside over bigger budgets in an illegal drugs climate. In this covert market products are sold without proper identification, industry controls, manufacturer name, usage instructions, safety cautions, or any buyer's guarantee or maker's liability. In a free market, the insurer's requirements and legal liabilities for makers of crack cocaine and heroin could be a lot more effective at inhibiting this drug's usage than are the ineffective efforts of police and politicians.

In a free and informed drugs market, fewer would choose the dangerous drugs. The evidence supports this in liberal countries such as Spain and Holland, where the majority of drug users choose from the far less toxic cannabis, ecstasy, mushrooms, and LSD. Many of these users have at one time or another sampled drugs such as cocaine, heroin, crack, meth-amphetamines, speed, or alcohol and either not returned, or just occasionally revisited. People are able to make intelligent choices, and when they are enjoying life, they are naturally interested in preserving their own, and act accordingly. Many of those minority who do slide downhill into a dangerous or damaging addiction will eventually pull themselves back, sometimes stronger for the experience. Alcoholics Anonymous has now been joined by Narcotics Anonymous. Legality isn't the issue. Yet the state steadfastly refuses to let us exercise our own judgment in drug use. We live in a world where if you choose to make up your own mind about what you do with it, you can go to jail—for your own good, of course.

This perverse small-minded attitude has embroiled much of the world in a virtual third World War under the guise of America's internationally exported War on Drugs. Whole economies have been ravaged and vast sums are spent each year from our taxes, and confiscated from our citizens, while the numbers imprisoned worldwide would equal the annual casualties of a great ongoing war. Millions of lives have been damaged to no purpose. This de facto World War does not defend us from any great evil threatening society. Yet it costs the US over $15 billion per year, fattening the coffers of those waging it—from the countless worldwide bureaus, agencies, and police forces, to the ever-expanding prison industry and makers of sophisticated testing apparatus. We frequently hear retired police chiefs, judges, and drug squad officers voicing the opinion that the War on Drugs is a failure, an opinion underlined by most major studies undertaken on the subject. Ex-President Bill Clinton is one of the latest to sing from the same "what a waste" song sheet.

> *The quality of life for all of us has been diminished by the growth of the police state and by the murderous activities of the criminal gangs enfranchised, and kept in business, by the blind and mindless perpetuation of this failed and bankrupt "War on Drugs."*
>
> Graham Hancock, author and speaker, 1950–

Perhaps the zeal with which this war is waged reflects the state's own dependency on the massive tax revenues it raises from the well-established approved drugs, and hinges on its cozy centuries-long relationship with distillers, tobacco companies, and the pharmaceutical industry—the biggest drug dealers in the world. The small cartels running these empires are accustomed to having a de facto monopoly on recreational drugs as well as medicinal or healing ones, seeing any other drugs, first and foremost, as unwanted competition.

Another prime stimulus to the intolerance of psychedelic drugs, and a more deeply rooted one, arises from a religious establishment fearing that personal revelations of brotherhood and oneness with the Universe might not be in accordance with church teachings. The world's three major prophet-driven religions cannot cope with the concept of spiritual understanding arising in us without the need for their books and stories (instructive as they may be). Could this be what the serpent offered us in the Garden of Eden? Taste of this fruit and ye shall taste what it is to be divine, and know the difference between good and evil (no mention of sex). Is this not a valuable thing to do? The gnostic Ophite sect, thriving in the first few centuries AD, had a similar biblical story, and in theirs the serpent was revered for offering us this sacred experience, and Jehova reviled for denying access and spurning the serpent. The Ophites were virtually erased from history by the triumphant Christian onslaught that soon followed its merger with the Roman Empire in the fourth century.

The casualties of the global War on Drugs are many and varied. Most obvious are those hundreds of thousands of the world's citizens who are locked up, at our expense, for indulging or trading in alternatives to the standard "OK by the USA" drug; substances like alcohol, tobacco, anti-depressants, sedatives, coffee, and cola drinks that must be the only mood or mind-altering fare available to the world. Though it has long been openly acknowledged that the majority of illegal drug shipments do get through to their markets, the casualties and costs continue to mount with no benefit for society. In the US it can cost upwards of $50,000 annually to house a convict, in addition to the cost of arrest, trial, and conviction, which can easily exceed $150,000. With just 5 percent of the world's population, the US holds 25 percent of those in prison globally. In other words, in the "land of the free" there are five times as many people in jail per capita as there are in the rest of the world.

Another level of casualties in the War on Drugs evolves from the distortion of the natural market, as consumers are driven to use and abuse more dangerous drugs than they would choose in a free market. The laws banning production, sale, and use of cannabis and ecstasy (MDMA) carry more responsibility for the growing abuse of cocaine than do all the drug barons of Colombia. They also carry responsibility for solvent-related deaths, teenage alcoholism, and the growing and dangerous abuse of pharmaceutical cocktail combinations that now figure as a major, though under-reported, problem in much of the US. Backflow occurred too, in the War on Drugs, when in the early 1980s the CIA are believed to have helped distribute crack cocaine to America's inner cities in order to covertly fund the Nicaraguan contras. History will undoubtedly judge that the War on Drugs was itself the largest causative factor of America's downhill slide into dangerous drug abuse. This would not be the first time that coercive state programs have produced opposite results to those intended. This war has clogged courts and jails worldwide with drug cases, creating far more problems than drugs ever posed on their own.

Like the American Prohibition of alcohol in the 1920s, the long-running War on Drugs has no chance whatsoever of success. As we know from history, the effect of Prohibition was to double the overall level of alcohol consumption while increasing deaths from sub-standard illicit alcohol. It provided the mafia with a very successful start in life and a database of virtually every club, bar, or place of entertainment in the US. And when marijuana prohibition ends, it could leave us the legacy of wealthy Mexican gangs controlling most of the American market, as do Vietnamese gangs in the UK. Prohibition provides us with an excellent example of the unintended consequences that arise from attempts to control society through top-down regulations underwritten by force.

> *The prestige of government has undoubtedly been lowered considerably by the prohibition law. For nothing is more destructive of respect for the government and the law of the land than passing laws which cannot be enforced.*
>
> Albert Einstein, theoretical physicist, 1879–1955

Society does have a problem with drug use. It is a serious problem that is getting worse. For some reason, though, the perception of this problem is focused entirely on the very small range of drugs that are being used illegally. We cannot ignore the very real problems faced by those who are using drugs prescribed by doctors. Their lives can be damaged and sometimes destroyed as a result of diagnostic error, their own abuse of the prescribed stocks (few recreational drug users have a month's supply in a bottle), or just years of being dependent on pharmaceuticals with known side effects. These legal drugs must be obtained through controlled channels, but these channels translate into a multi-billion dollar industry throughout the world—the real drugs trade. While we condemn it when drug barons bribe and seduce judges, police, and politicians, we think nothing of the lobbyists employed by the pharmaceutical industry in Washington DC, who number more than three for every single Congressman or Senator. To rephrase that, there are 535 elected representatives shaping law and regulation in the capital of the United States, attended to by 1,724 paid persuaders from the pharmaceutical drug barons alone (as well as some 9,750 lobbyists from other interest groups in 2011).

The most successful, and profitable, pharmaceutical drugs are those which do not cure, but instead create a lifelong habit for the user, such as steroids, beta blockers, and antihistamines. These often generate hundreds or even thousands of dollars/pounds a month income to the suppliers. These drug dealers' lobbyists openly encourage the state to pass laws controlling and restricting the alternative healing industry and the sale of herbal and other natural and unpatented medicinal remedies. Their expert lobbyists put convincing arguments to politicians that herbal medicines are unsafe and endanger the user's life, over a nice cardiac-endangering lunch at a top restaurant. Even the deadly killers alcohol and tobacco are usually left out of the picture when the vast majority talk about "the drug problem."

While acknowledging the dangers posed by some illegal drugs, I point out that the unnecessary suffering and destruction meted out by the "authorized" drugs trade is clearly the greater problem, despite being managed by trained people in white coats and slick PR professionals. More people will probably die from mis-applied or mis-prescribed pharmaceuticals in a week than from the so-called drug problem in a year. The statistics are not released and possibly not even tallied.

Changing our state of mind has long been a normal part of human activity, whatever agent or activity is being used to bring about the change. To allow some techniques, dangerous and addictive ones, as it happens, and ban others is an unacceptable intervention in our evolution. Many of these drugs arise from the vegetable kingdom, having specific fits to receptors in our brain that are designed to recognize and respond to their presence. The freedom to exercise sovereignty over our own state of mind should be at the core of any society calling itself free, and we must openly recognize and reject the audacity of those who would deny it us.

Disclaimer: *Readers are advised to avoid all illegal drugs and to only ever ingest those substances that have been approved by the government, or prescribed by a government-approved doctor. Then you will be a happy, healthy bunny.*

28

Positive Protest: Get Fluffy!
(The Roots of Seattle)

Photo taken by this author at the 1997 Reclaim The Streets party, held in London's Trafalgar Square. The following year saw scores of RTS parties staged across the country and around the world.

It is the growing perception of many on this planet that as we begin the 21st century, our society and civilization could be compared to a ship that is slowly sinking, or is in such rough waters that sinking is a distinct possibility. Some in our society are trying to repair the damage, building organizations and developing new lifestyles that do not threaten the planet. The state often reacts by passing laws to hamper activity of this sort, while issuing blanket assurances that all is well. It sometimes seems like the state is banning the construction of lifeboats and drilling little holes in the ones that have already been constructed. When the state does acknowledge a problem, its solutions often aggravate the situation, as is so clearly the case with its support of bio-fuels and nuclear power.

Whether they are correct or not, those who feel a sense of responsibility for our civilization will react to this perceived danger by considering and experimenting with alternative lifestyles and prompting change to the status quo. They will also seek to make their voices heard over the blind assurances of the state that everything is being done for our own good and with our approval, since some of us voted for those who are making the decisions (or against their opponents).

To sin by silence when they should protest makes cowards of men.

Abraham Lincoln, 1809–1865

Were it not for those who perceive problems before they become tragedies, society would indeed have a very rocky road to follow. Though predictors of impending disaster are not always right, they should be heard and considered. Many who did get it right were silenced. Why is it that every nuclear accident or release of toxins to the environment is accompanied by the familiar voice of the state assuring us that there has been no risk to public health or safety? As long as there is a seven-year-old inner-city child alive without asthma, we will be told by straight-faced government scientists that there is no "scientific proof" of a connection between increasing air pollution and rising asthma levels in children.

We vitally need the early warnings of those who are often dismissed as scaremongers, cranks, or just "not like us" troublemakers. We have many examples of whistleblowers who were attacked and undermined for their discoveries and revelations. Rachel Carson, who exposed the dangers of pesticides in 1962 with her bestselling *Silent Spring,* was a rare case who fought back and won, leading to the banning of DDT in much of the world. Dr. John Yudkin was successfully discredited in the 70s after scientifically explaining, in his book *Pure, White and Deadly,* just how dangerous an addition sugar was to the human diet. Dr. Richard Lacy was discredited and sidelined in the 80s for warning of Mad Cow Disease; the eminent Dr. Pusztai's career ended in 1998 when he discovered damage done to rats through eating GM potatoes, and publicized it. In 2009, Dr. David Nutt lost his job as chair of the UK government's drug advisory body for stating that cannabis is not a dangerous drug. Julian Assange, the great provider and platform for whistleblowers worldwide, lives locked within Ecuador's London embassy at the time of writing, not charged with any crime but wanted for questioning in Sweden.

Silence becomes cowardice when occasion demands speaking out the whole truth and acting accordingly.

Mahatma Gandhi, 1869–1948

Throughout history, countless crucial discoveries, understandings, and revelations have been mocked and suppressed before eventually becoming part of the accepted wisdom. My brother Craig and I were mocked by many for advocating, in the 60s, that what we eat affects our health. We urgently need pioneers, scientists, and whistleblowers with the courage to speak their minds, exposing duplicity and evil in an open climate without risking assault by the state or the status quo. Most, possibly all, of the state's monitoring networks are staffed by scientists and researchers bound to official secrecy, expressly forbidden from blowing any whistles when they discover contaminants in our food and environment. Their bosses have the choice of whether or not any purpose is served by alerting the public, those nondescript people paying their salaries.

Nothing strengthens authority so much as silence.

Leonardo da Vinci, 1452–1519

As nation states throughout the world have become more oppressive in their ways, we have seen a disturbing move to violence among those who seek to make their voice heard above the status quo's attempts to silence dissent. Protest becomes frightening when demonstrators with twisted faces throw bricks and bottles while shouting obscenities at the armored and uniformed agents of the state. Such behavior is alien to most and clouds our perception of the issues as we seek to distance ourselves from the ugliness of those making the case. However, after the Gandhi-inspired Campaign for Nuclear Disarmament (CND) was unable to halt the mad proliferation of nuclear arms in the 1960s, many lost hope that nonviolent protest was a vehicle for change and either gave up, approached it from a fresh new angle, or joined an extreme group of left or right.

Yet something very new and very powerful arose in Britain during the 1990s. A new culture developed that was able to stage peaceful acts of dramatic civil disobedience that would have had Thoreau, Tolstoy, and Gandhi dancing in their graves. Compared to the singing, or just lie-down-and-go-limp tactics used by the CND movement of the early 1960s, these new and aptly termed "eco-warriors" had advanced from the bow and arrow to the laser-guided smart bomb—if you will forgive the analogy. In the warrior tradition, they set strategies together, acting either in concert or individually on the field of play. It soon became police practice to assemble a ratio of five police to one eco-warrior before commencing any action. One of the foundations of this new protest power lay in the attitude initially defined by the word "fluffy," describing a nonviolent approach to dealing in face-to-face, fearless defiance of the full power of the state. It is not a passive strategy, and having fun is an important part of it. Regardless of where your thoughts lie on the roads issue, it is here that "nonviolent direct action" (NVDA, the technical term that has all but replaced "fluffy") was fashioned into an effective working tool that has spread across the world; most recently underlying some of the core principles in the Occupy movement. The coercive state may never develop a means to successfully "deal with" nonviolent behavior to its satisfaction. So how did it come into existence?

> *Disobedience is the true foundation of liberty. The obedient must be slaves.*

> Henry David Thoreau, 1817–1862

The first spark of this inspired new take on NVDA came in 1993 at the spontaneous obstruction of a proposed road scheme across Twyford Down, England. A group of concerned people visiting the proposed new road site became appalled by the thoughtlessness with which the countryside was about to be destroyed for automobiles and were inspired to set up the country's first positively staged protest against a road. They came to call themselves the Dongas tribe, after the ancient paths and rights-of-way that were once an integral part of that land. The final eviction, a black milestone in Britain's history, involved four days of often brutal and violent removal by police and security forces, against a dedicated and spirited resistance by the Dongas. Twyford Down was soon followed by a passionate and prolonged battle to prevent a bypass destroying the beautiful Solsbury Hill outside of Bath, which sadly is no longer there to enjoy.

Veterans of these first two anti-road building confrontations came to London, setting the stage for the historic urban No-M11 Link Campaign. This was to evolve into a multi-headed nonviolent and non-hierarchical campaign against the destruction of our planet, spreading throughout Britain and eventually across the oceans.

The yearlong No-M11 action involved the peaceful occupation and fortification of Claremont Road, the final street of residential houses waiting to be bulldozed for a three-mile motorway link of dubious value. The link would devour a longstanding neighborhood of three hundred houses to shave three minutes off commuter time. Most of the original residents had been forced to sell and move out but a few held on defiantly. New neighbors soon joined them, as squatters opposed to the building of the bypass occupied the empty houses. Claremont Road rapidly became a lively community of people with two inexpensive vegetarian cafes and more exciting innovative art than you would see at the Edinburgh Festival. A small flat-bed truck was transformed into a stage, supporting regular musical events and street parties. All this with no demands for rent, though a high demand for courage, innovation, DIY culture, and tolerance.

One of the road's many iconic art works

RUST IN PEACE

At the final siege on November 28, 1994, after well over a year's occupation, some two hundred entrenched eco-warriors occupied twelve houses facing 1,400 invaders. Using strictly fluffy tactics, they held out against an army of seven hundred heavily equipped police, three hundred bailiffs, and four hundred security guards for five long days and nights. This dramatic final siege and eviction was accompanied by minimal scenes of violence or ugly confrontation, one injury from a fall, and this author being carried in his wheelchair along the length of the street by four goons with "Sheriff" written on their backs.

For the first few days, a well-concealed tunnel had supplied energy and essential supplies to the besieged protesters. The final defender to be taken was Phil, not burrowing deep in a tunnel, but plucked from his sleep atop the splendid Dolly's Tower, built with fluorescent scaffolding rising seventy feet above the short row of houses. It was named after Dolly, the sharp and lucid ninety-two-year-old darling who had refused to leave her lifelong home ("They'll have to carry me out"—and they did). She regarded her unconventional new neighbors as modern heroes, fighting today's Battle of Britain against the mindless destruction of our habitat and history by road-building schemes that are often ill-thought-out, frivolous, or downright unnecessary. Many others in the local neighbourhood shared Dolly's views and gave their full support and love to the new community in their midst.

The now footloose ex-residents of Claremont Road took their empowering and inspired techniques with them, taught others, and transformed into a multi-headed Hydra. Protesters began staging unpredictable, theatrical, nonviolent, and humorous actions across the country, all dedicated to respecting our environment. In between they were busy setting up new communities in road-threatened woodlands, buildings awaiting eventual demolition, and on wasteland, common land, and in premises selected from the abundant stock of unused state-owned buildings (old courthouses, social security offices, unused schools). Sometimes long-vacant private properties or land are squatted as well. Here they would seek, and sometimes obtain, the owner's permission to remain, on the understanding that they would take care of the building and vacate it at short notice. In 2012 legislation was introduced which has now curtailed squatting in long-vacant private homes. (The ethics of squatting may sit uncomfortably with many readers, as it would with this writer were not cases of its abuse infrequent. In those "primitive" cultures that recognized owning the right to use land, but not ownership of the land itself, there existed customs that saw someone lose rights to the exclusive use of land which had for a period of years neither been enjoyed by them nor their tenants—left vacant and unattended.)

One of the most audacious spinoffs from the No-M11 Campaign, in 1995, was the low-profile group of activists calling themselves Reclaim the Streets (RTS). They acquired a reputation for pulling off the impossible—stomping daytime street parties in major urban roads. The intention was to apply a brake to the paving over of the planet. For many, the most memorable of these was "Street Party '96," which had its own flyers distributed across Britain many weeks in advance. People came from afar. What was the fluffy spirit of Claremont Road to achieve here? Nothing less than a giant unauthorized (illegal) street party at an undisclosed major London road location, attended by eight thousand positive party-goers—all right under the eyes of the police authorities, in spite of their very determined efforts to stop this party from taking place.

The day before the party only four people knew its location; by two o'clock the next afternoon over six thousand were either at or on their way to the 800-meter-long M41 Westway link in west London's Shepherd's Bush. All six lanes in both directions were smoothly occupied, in a precision action coordinating a truckload of sand "broken down" in the lay-by, the sound system truck likewise, a cavalry of a hundred or more cyclists, a few quickly erected tripods with people suspended therein, and thousands of party-goers simultaneously pouring in from nearby tube stations, having originally all assembled at Liverpool St. Station on the other side of London.

Once the party kicked off, the police did an efficient and good-natured job of redirecting traffic for the afternoon and evening (with a fraction of the disturbance caused by a single IRA bomb scare). They never donned their riot outfits but quipped, "Thanks for coming, hope you had a good time," to me and many others as we left around midnight. There were caterers keeping us fed, plenty of wandering entertainers, a children's play area, carpets thrown down for sitting, and a high proportion of the non-status quo attending. There were two giant Mardi Gras-style moving ballroom gown constructions, moved by a small team beneath the skirt. One of these settled next to the throbbing sound system for the evening and, as the police helicopter hovered overhead, a pneumatic drill worked away under cover of its skirts and the nearby repetitive beat. Its purpose was to plant a tree in the fast lane of the motorway—a strongly poetic statement and better than the usual arsenal of nastiness. It was difficult for the agents of coercion to deal with such non-aggressive and doggedly determined opponents with nothing to lose—something that their police training had not covered. There was no violence and just one arrest—of the man handing out leaflets suggesting we do something rude to the Queen.

Many new camps arose and several fluffy "universities" were established, teaching the techniques learned at Claremont Road and other actions. This new wave of protesters was soon joined by the older and respectable population of Middle England who shared concern over the loss of countryside. My own father, when visiting Claremont Road, compared it to his childhood neighborhood in 1920s Bridgeville, Pennsylvania, where everybody knew each other and shared life as a community.

Another major offshoot of Claremont Road was the historic Third Battle of Newbury—waged without violence against the controversial and poorly planned Newbury Bypass route. Between July 1995 and January 1996 thirty-six separate camps were built in the path of the proposed route, complete with tree houses, lock-ons, aerial walkways, kitchens, communication facilities, and all the other artifacts of this new mobile community. Many Newbury locals became involved, with both police and security guards frequently expressing their support for the protesters' position. It eventually took a hugely costly, often laughable, and sometimes frightening operation by the authorities to exert their will and secure access to the site for building contractors Costain. Private security guards, apparently paid directly from Whitehall, had access to confidential police records and conducted surveillance reminiscent of that practiced behind the former Iron Curtain. Phone taps, infiltration, and all the usual tools of the covert state were much in evidence.

Soon after the 360 acres of ancient Newbury woodland, Ten thousand trees, historic battlefields, and thirty-six protest camps along the route had been taken and leveled, the Minister of Transport responsible at the time admitted publicly that the road protesters had it right and that the Newbury bypass should never have been built along that route. From the safety of retirement, he acknowledged that the well over-due U-Turn in this country's roads policy had been brought about in just a few years by direct action road protest. Though most of the individual battle-stands of this campaign have eventually fallen before the weight of the coercive state, it was at Newbury that the war appeared to have been won.

Other fluffy actions have included the giant canvas mock motorway somehow draped over the then transport minister's house in the early morning. In protest at the police state powers granted by the Criminal Justice Act, a "mystery excursion" brought several busloads to a picnic held in the garden of the Home Secretary's country house, then held and videoed a mock trial in which he was found guilty on various counts. In another anti-CJA action, five audacious men scaled the rooftop of the Houses of Parliament on the eve of Guy Fawkes Night. Profiled against Big Ben, they unfurled a large banner, smoked a large joint, and called the press on their mobile phone, coming down only as the cold rainy night progressed. No charges were made following any of the above actions.

The fluffy approach to NVDA does not see people of any type as an enemy just because they wear a particular uniform, are a different color, or practice a strange religion. Fluffy tries to not invite baton charges nor incurs them in most instances. Nonviolent and playful behavior is recognized to work better than violence and that is why it has become established as the preferred modus operandi for a new breed of action-oriented bell-ringers. Even the police show it increasing respect as they realize that they are unlikely to ever confront brick-throwing, punching, or even verbal abuse with a response stronger than "Get a real job," "Shame on you!" or "What will your grandchildren think?"

At the center of nonviolence stands the principle of love.

Martin Luther King, Jr., 1929–1968

Today's eco-warriors display a constant level of inspiration and innovation, evolving techniques that can sometimes be likened to those of the martial art of T'ai Chi Chuan, in which a minimum of graceful movement takes the opponent's energy and turns it back with even greater force. It is combined with a powerful commitment to a DIY culture, which takes personal responsibility for tasks in hand, without any defined leadership or hierarchical control structure (originally, DIY referred to do-it-yourself home improvements, and now applies also to a self-responsible lifestyle outside the mainstream).

Humor, including the ability to laugh at the totalitarian aspirations of the state while sticking a soft spanner in its works, seems to achieve better results than outrage and paranoia. It certainly maintains morale, raised spirits, and higher energy in its practitioners, and garners greater support from the public. Many of the techniques and tactics developed by this fluffy philosophy are intended to disable the adrenal glands and confuse the responses of those who are sent to attack them. The protesters seek to treat the police, bailiffs, or security guards as human beings rather than the enemy. For some reason, this confuses them.

NVDA is having an effect on the mainstream culture as millions of so-called ordinary citizens realize that valid points are being made by articulate and committed people, without using violence to gain attention. A major scaling down of superfluous road schemes has taken place, and their future development will never be quite so carefree again. General awareness has risen on the issues of air pollution, urban sprawl, animal welfare, nuclear power, and our shrinking personal freedoms. When the full costs of some of this period's follies are counted by future generations, I do not wonder who will be looked upon as the villains and who as the heroes.

> *Never be afraid to raise your voice for honesty and truth*
> *and compassion against injustice and lying and greed.*
> *If people all over the world . . .would do this, it would*
> *change the earth.*

> William Faulkner, American writer and Nobel Laureate,
> 1897–1962

In response to this new style of protest, the British state passed—and continues to draft—extremely repressive legislation designed to make criminal any aspects of Britain's emerging new culture of which it disapproves. The Criminal Justice Bill of 1994 was carefully designed to suppress techno music parties, the right to assembly, the right to protest, and anything else that the state found irritating or embarrassing. Techno music was legally described as "wholly or predominantly characterized by the emission of a succession of repetitive beats." Look out, Bach lovers—you might be next.

Kate Evans Postcard

Soon, the rubber-stamped Police Act of 1997 extended police powers of surveillance, allowing them to bug or burgle anybody they suspect to be guilty of the "serious offense" of being one of "a large number of persons in pursuit of a common purpose." Really! The police were also given power to close clubs on the basis of a suspicion that somebody might be taking illegal drugs inside. Britain's subsequent rulers, rather than rolling back some of this tyranny, have instead further extended their rights to suppress dissent and monitor their citizens' private communications and online activity. The United States and many other modern states continue to erode our hard-won human rights in the name of preserving our safety.

I believe there are more instances of the abridgement of freedom of the people by gradual and silent encroachments by those in power than by violent and sudden usurpations.

James Madison, Founding Father and US President,
1751–1836

Typically, the effect of the Criminal Justice Bill and associated legislation was not exactly what the government intended. It served instead to connect up the hundreds of different groups at which it was targeted and to spawn thousands more. At one point the British group LIBERTY was registering nine new groups being formed every day in opposition to the bill's passage. The "movement," or whatever you choose to call it, became stronger and more networked than ever before.

In 1998, the world's first anti-globalization protest party was organized by RTS in Birmingham. There, we peacefully obstructed the intended G8 summit by launching a party in the centrally strategic Bull Ring Roundabout complex, blocking access from delegates' hotels to the conference center. It was a damn good party, and the sole wanton violence we witnessed was a young man gassed with CS by a policeman for no good reason. Since then such events have regularly prompted similar activities throughout the world, with the "Battle for Seattle" propelling this new form and focus of protest into the world's headlights. I was heartened to discover that the socially conscious Occupy Wall Street participants re-grouped after Hurricane Sandy in 2012. They rapidly became one of the most effective distributors of assistance and aid to the worst affected areas, receiving official recognition for their contribution.

This enhanced new approach to having fun while promoting peaceful change has spread worldwide, strengthened by Internet connectivity and supported by smart technology acting as the people's CCTV, for instant broadcast. The state's fundamental resource is the threat of force, and it is pointless for those opposing it to engage with the state on that playing field. So we match force with the only thing we are stronger in, which is ingenuity and playful fun aimed at bringing out and nurturing the humanity of the human species. That's a potent weapon, and increasingly the one of choice for those seeking to reverse the damage being inflicted upon our world and the global community.

> *Nonviolence is the greatest force at the disposal of mankind. It is mightier than the mightiest weapon of destruction devised by the ingenuity of man.*
>
> Mahatma Gandhi, 1869–1948

Disclaimer: *Readers are advised not to take part in any activities, gatherings, parties, or protests proscribed by the Criminal Justice Act 1994, or any other official regulation. If you really want to be happy in life, then just stick to the rules, do what you're told, and don't try thinking for yourself.*

29

A Working Example

I have made much of society's ability to rise to the challenge of providing for its needs non-coercively, when free to do so. I have also sought to convince you to overcome fear of the void—to let go of your own inability as an individual to imagine the complex structures that would fill the holes left by the state's ineptitude and eventual decline.

It is not the remit of this book to conceive or predict the structures that will be necessary to replace the state's failing services, but let me take an example from the past, which I have already mentioned once or twice. I refer to an industry that would be impossible to imagine if it did not already exist; which provides just the sort of service that we would expect our government to provide. This industry has managed to make a profit at it since it began in earnest several centuries ago. It is a different type of organization from most and at its highest level does not employ limited liability as a defense against mistakes or incompetence.

Have you guessed it yet, or do you take the insurance business so much for granted that you never thought much about it? Or perhaps you never thought enough about insurance to realize how special it is, instead holding the not uncommon view that it is peopled by unprincipled scavengers feeding off the misfortunes of the human race. What insurance actually does is buy your risks, worries, and fears from you. Since you view these things as being negative in value, their "price" has a minus sign in front, so you pay them instead of the other way around. You can actually buy a product that provides for your family if you die, buys you a new car if the one you spent five years' savings for gets totaled, or supplies top-grade wigs and compensation for any customers going bald with your hair shampoo. You can insure against it raining on your outdoor festival or against breaking your nose if you are a supermodel. Incredible service, isn't it? And one you purchase in the hope that you will never have to use it.

This industry didn't develop as a result of any government initiative or ruling. It arose instead from our inherent ability to create social and enterprise structures that play a part in governing our lives. At its simplest level, the concept was embodied in the communal grain store of a pre-industrial village, providing insurance against famine. In many earlier cultures, members of a community would unite to rebuild a house if one had been lost to fire or storm. Ancient Chinese and Babylonian traders had techniques for insuring against the potential losses of cargos and ships. An element of insurance was built into the culture of the Zoroastrian Persian Empire. It's a great concept.

The modern insurance industry traces its origins back to fourteenth century Genoa, with the invention of simple insurance policies covering maritime loss. It came of age in the late seventeenth century, prompted by two events. The Great Fire of London in 1666 inspired one Nicholas Barbon to offer fire insurance on brick and frame buildings, the first building insurance. Then in 1688 Edward Lloyd opened an establishment where ship owners, merchants, and wealthy risk-takers gathered to indulge in one of their regular cargoes, a popular new drug called coffee. Lloyd's of London evolved to become a thriving worldwide market for maritime insurance and retains its leading position to this day. The presence of Lloyd's in London supported England's rise to become a great maritime trading nation by enabling entrepreneurs to take risks without risking being wiped out. It was a small cost of business since most ships and cargoes did come through.

I will not go into detail on the mechanics that enable this industry to maintain enough money to cover and spread the risks they promise to cover, without squandering most of it on administration and overheads. I will not dwell on the exceptional cases we hear of, when insurers have dishonored the spirit of their contracts. But I will make the point that the insurance industry does not benefit from hurricanes, lightning strikes, sunken ships, car crashes, or cancer diagnoses. The worldwide insurance industry that covers our risks in life willingly pays out billions every year to enable the rebuilding of lives, homes, factories, farms, and dreams that have been destroyed by the unpredictable. It is a broad-based social service that works, that rapidly evolves to cover new types of risk, and that manages to do so in a self-sustaining manner without the need to force our money from us. When insurers pay a claim, we are not made to feel like some supplicant receiving their blessing. The insurance industry is not perfect—but it continues to survive and evolve by serving a purpose, as does everything else in the natural world. This industry is used as an example specifically because it does just the sort of thing that the state would have us believe only it can do. And it could do more, which we will touch upon in the next chapter.

Today, as we consider the many problems facing society and the natural world, we are most often channeled into a fruitless and frustrating stagger down a one-way street. When the discussion turns to subjects like crime, education, health, homelessness, or pollution, we end up thinking within the framework of the state since it is all we have ever known. The problem is addressed in terms of the proposed legislation, restrictions, and subsidies supported by either the In Party or the Out party—or the regulations that would be imposed if sensible people like us were in charge of things. We delve again and again into the "terminal tool bag" of the state, looking for a magic way to make these devices work. This is because we accept that the state has the right to manage these areas, expecting them to eventually lead us forward rather than hold us back. We must now embrace alternative options, figuring out what we ourselves can do, as did those ship owners and merchants at Lloyd's Coffee House. We do not need to predict or determine exactly what form a new concept will have assumed after two, twenty, or two hundred years of evolution from the original idea. We can be sure, though, that as we recognize new needs, the solutions will be sought and developed.

Never in the planet's history has a single species been more interconnected as a community than today. The information technology now available and the personal power that it gives us make self-management of our complex society, on a global level, a more real and attainable concept than it has ever been.

30

The Ways and Means

Liberty means responsibility. That is why most men dread it.

George Bernard Shaw, 1856–1950

This book never set out to offer answers for all the challenges that will face us as the state's services deteriorate or cease altogether. But as we have seen in many areas of human endeavor, society is adept at developing the mechanisms that meet its needs, often providing the sort of services that we might imagine require a central state. People, not the state, got things moving when they built canals, railroads, airlines, subways, and bus networks. People, not the state, brought us together with telegraph, telephones and wi-fi, laying cables across oceans and sending satellines into orbit. The British Coast Guard service is entirely staffed by volunteers using boats supplied by the charity RNLI. Most rural firefighting stations across the US are locally organized and operated by volunteers. We are community-building animals and good at it.

This chapter puts forward some "imaginings" of overall governing structures or principles that are well within the means of our society to manage. These structures might develop in a climate where needs arise in society—needs which are no longer the exclusive preserve of the state to manage. It should even be possible to build some of them alongside the state's faltering structures.

The most universal and essential product group of all is the food that we eat, usually more than once every day of our lives, regardless of where we live. Of course we need standards for our foods so we can guard against botulism in canned food and be sure that the ingredients listed on a food packet are complete and accurate. We want to know that when a product is labeled as organically grown, it fits a valid criteria for "organic." And we want to be sure that our food is not contaminated with heavy metals, toxic bacteria, rat droppings, radioactive particles, pesticides, unexpected forms of flesh, hormone residues, or other noxious contaminants.

Though the state would have us believe that it looks after all the above and more, today's increasingly conscious consumers are becoming ever more aware of the flimsiness of the state's protection—a state whose own involvement in the food chain has led to dangers far more endemic and frightening than rat droppings or even a touch of heavy metal. Typically the state will try to deny or cover up its own dangerous mistakes, assuring us that there has been no risk to human health. Occasionally, when scientists speak out about the dangers, they will suggest that consumers, if they want to be absolutely sure, should consume fewer farmed salmon, or be sure to peel their potatoes and apples, while not suggesting they be overly concerned. Then, one suspects, they will take steps to ensure that such information does not unexpectedly leak out again in the future, and wait for things to get back to abnormal.

Where consumers are unconcerned about their food quality, no amount of regulations will make much difference to the quality of their diet—a diet that has often been downgraded by government interference in the food chain. Today, as consumers increasingly appreciate the connection between their health and the foods with which they make and power themselves, a vacuum exists for a company whose remit is to provide genuine certification to food producers, incorporating regular testing of their products and verification of claims made for products. This can be done with bonded personnel able to review, among many other factors, a company's working recipes, relative to ingredient listing. It will be in the long-term interests of the food industry to have a standard of integrity that can be trusted by the public.

If such a standard is developed and maintained by a private organization, its very existence would be threatened were integrity lost by colluding with a food company over false data. Today there is always the chance of such activity being exposed online or on Twitter, TV, or by the press. Such a certification mark adds value to the product and would be paid for by a modest charge to the company based on volume or value. There can be alternative validation schemes available so, for instance, separate companies may deal with organic or cruelty-free claims from those validating ingredient and nutritional contents. Since the first incarnation of this book, the Fairtrade Mark has grown hugely in popularity, as well as the certification of organically grown products from wine to ice cream and cotton to kitchen furniture, plus brown rice and olive oil. In practice, it does work.

The intention here is not to map out the specifics of how such a company might run or how it might deal with all the ifs and buts that any critic of such a concept would raise. Let's also not pretend we are so stupid that we would be confused by a jungle of different symbols. Such an industry is by its nature likely to standardize, though it may (or may not) begin with a confusing array of symbols. In the author's experience, however, when a consumer seeks to be assured that a product is vegetarian, Kosher, or fairly produced, then that consumer is willing to look for the symbol. Something similar has developed in the travel industry, without government intervention, with an international coding that lets you know everything about a hotel from the number of beds, to disabled access, to swimming pool, golf course, Internet connection, and catering facilities. The ultimate mark for the food industry would be one that simply verifies that all the manufacturer's claims (fair trade, vegan, 100 percent beef, sugar free, organic, gluten free, Kosher, low fat, high in Omega 3) are true, correct, and not misleading.

Naturally, in the absence of state control, such a scheme would not be a mandatory requirement for all food manufacturers. Many retailers would choose to demand it of their large suppliers while performing in-house vetting of the small manufacturers, who keep supermarket shelves interesting and changing (and are easier to inspect at one small unit). Some brands' credentials might be so beyond reproach as to not need any outside standard, though such a manufacturer may proudly be the scheme's keen supporter. What we achieve with this service is another important weave added to the web of our food supply system, providing rapid feedback from the public to the food suppliers about the changing needs and perceptions of that society. This is not something that management by the state can ever provide.

In the same way, we are perfectly capable as a society of developing standards and means to ensure that our cigarette lighters do not explode, that our cars run at the promised MPG, that dye-fast clothes do not run, or that babies' mattresses do not explode into flames. While there should be no restrictions on appointing whomever we like (including ourselves) to act in "professional" areas for us, we are able to ensure through various accreditations or associations that our lawyer, doctor, publisher, architect, or plumber has met certain standards of responsibility and expertise that we desire. Of course, we are often likely to be swayed by a good reputation and personal recommendation, but valid certification is always reassuring. Though often obstructed by jealous state control of standards, we should soon see an even greater development of independent product certification companies providing customer guarantees with responsibility.

No standards are of much use without a form of written codes and regulations that govern the action to be taken in the case of their willful or accidental transgression. Let us look at civil law for now, which often does not involve coercion but requires some form of redress for damage, injury, poor service, or break of guarantee. It is quite possible for a system to evolve whereby companies and individuals trading in goods and services voluntarily associate themselves with a large Assurance House that sets and maintains codes of conducts and regulation applying to their interactions; companies abide by this or they lose their reputation and ability to work within the business community. Integrity, guarantees, and liabilities can be financially backed by the Assurance House, which may require a security deposit from companies seeking to repair a shaky reputation. Support of this organization would be a basic cost of doing business for many, though street vendors, charity sales, startup enterprises, and others may choose not to be bonded, or to undertake some simpler and less all-inclusive scheme. But whatever transaction you are involved in, strive always to be aware. However convenient it is to have things looked after for us by others, we should never let our powers of discrimination completely decay or forget the old adage "let the buyer beware." Be aware.

The already vast mechanism of practical civil law, which includes the use of arbitrators, does not require the additional weight of the state to support and maintain itself. Most companies, large and small, work with an extensive base of existing contracts and codes that are accepted and expected. Some companies and people work on a simple handshake, knowing their honor is enough assurance. Others may draft long and devious contracts that "legally" cheat the other side out of what was expected, or will openly break the agreement and challenge the aggrieved party to try and sue for justice through the courts, at great expense. I do not intend to elaborate on how contracts could be guaranteed and the existing structure improved, other than that it must arise from within the trading community, and will need the appropriate types of assurance and bonding companies. Of course, we need honest banking for this to work—another horizon to aim for. I believe the need for this to be so great that a solution will arise within the commercial world in order to ensure the ongoing survival and effectiveness of trade. Much of the structure that is required already exists.

There is no limit to the ingenuity of man if it is properly and vigorously applied under conditions of peace and justice.

Winston Churchill, 1874–1964

Now let us take a fresh look, for a moment, at something that does not work very well in the "developed" world, which is the system of police, prisons, and judiciary that is responsible for handling the criminal element of our society. As touched upon earlier, this state-managed industry thrives on crime since ever more criminals create the need for ever more police, prisons, and lawyers, who inwardly assume crime to be an ever-growing problem. As an organism, of course, this is the industry's best growth and survival strategy. The invention of ever more victimless crimes is a natural result of such a structure—a system that verily feeds upon crime and grows along with it. Nobody gets rewarded if the police reduce crime, and with it the need for police, jails, and judges.

I expect that you have heard of the traditional Chinese doctor to whom you would pay small amounts regularly, but only while you were healthy and well. Payments stopped if you were sick and were only reinstated when you were restored to health. What about a police force that survives by getting paid regular small amounts when you are not threatened—and then has to foot the bill if a crime does take place that causes you a loss? Doesn't that sound great? It's actually more attainable than it seems. We already have two of the parts—they are just not connected. We pay a substantial amount in our taxes to fund a police force that is charged with preventing and solving crimes. That's one part. The other part was footing the bill when their failure allows crime to happen. The insurance companies do that, as we pay them regular small sums to cover the whole cost of whatever we choose to insure. They pay money out when a loss occurs, and even if you are murdered or hit by a bus right after you make that first monthly payment, they will foot the bill for the rest of your surviving partner's mortgage and for your children's education and upbringing. Believe me, they would be happier if you were still breathing. They have plenty of other things that people insure against, from bad weather to earthquakes to pianists' fingers.

So what might an alternate approach look like? Although it may not seem obvious, it is very much in the interest of the giant worldwide insurance industry to combat crime. The bulk of the industry supplies cover against risks of death, disaster, misfortunes, and unexpected events that involve no malevolent acts of mankind. As well as natural events, cover is also supplied against the risk of being robbed or injured in the course of a crime. Though some might argue that rising crime is good for the insurers because they get more policies from frightened people, we see this is starkly not the case in American inner-city areas where crime is so bad they will not insure. There is no joy at the insurance office when a client is robbed or murdered, or when crime figures rise—any more than there is glee at increased hurricanes, fires, bus crashes, or floods. When these events occur, so do a cost and a deduction from profits—when they occur too often, then the insurer may ultimately risk losing his or her shirt, since unlimited liability is the tradition at the top of the insurance ladder. Much of the industry growth today comes from new insurance such as that which covers breakage on the way home for items purchased on a credit card, or bad weather insurance for outdoor events, or other areas where there may not be any exploitation of your fear—just a means to offset a perfectly straightforward risk.

Since the main cost to insurance companies is payouts to customers who make claims, their greatest interest is in reducing the number of claims. The point being made is: when the insurance companies start to build tools with which to prevent crime and pursue criminals, they will not be victims of the "terminal tool bag" syndrome. They have nothing to gain from increasing crime and everything to gain from its reduction. They have nothing to gain from putting people in jail for crimes that have no victims, nor in putting the wrong people in jail just to secure a conviction. Indeed they have everything to gain from reducing the incidence of crimes with victims, and the need for expensive jails.

The insurance companies may need other allies from the business world, and it is not hard to recognize that, with the assistance of those involved in the financial system, it would be very difficult for criminals, once detected, to enjoy the proceeds of their crimes. The world of business must certainly recognize that society's desire for the reduction of crime and immorality is an opportunity for profit to themselves, greater in the long term than that afforded by its proliferation. I do not propose how this would work but have more hope of a solution being found in this arena than expectation of seeing crime reduced by further strengthening a coercively based justice industry that feeds on crime.

So if we get there, how do we stay there? Let us imagine that we have finally arrived at the idyllic situation where there are no coercive states in the world—nobody to threaten our now dissolved borders and forcibly dictate how we behave while emptying our pockets of as much as they can. So how, in this blissful peace, do we ensure that another Genghis Khan, Adolf Hitler, or Pol Pot does not secretly amass an army and arsenal of weapons with which to conquer the entire unarmed world? How can we prevent this without maintaining a large military force as deterrent—a force that could easily become that which we seek to deter?

However successfully insurance companies reduce crime, there will inevitably be the odd murder, but when we need to prevent an armed coercive state for birthing itself, we cannot risk a single occurrence. I am not about to lay out a 1-2-3 solution for doing this but observe that today we live in a surveillance state where all our phone use, travel, and online activity can be accessed in secret and assessed by shadowy operatives of a state that thrives on taxation. This same technology would exist in our borderless world of free people enjoying life in a joined-up, well-ordered, and naturally governed global community. That technology could rapidly detect early signs of criminals intent on state-building, spotting telltale communication patterns, weapons purchase or manufacture, recruiting activity, training programs, and so forth. In a culture where the intent to subjugate and rule over other people by force is viewed as the most serious crime imaginable, such activity could be halted without violence by the removal of essential services such as finance, communication, and power. We are imagining a world where companies and people who have a reputation for fair dealing, honesty, and reliability are those that do best and gain the greatest influence; a world where the tricksters and cheats didn't end up in control; a world of free people with industries that are independent, interdependent, and naturally connected by a network of feedback loops. It is a sad reflection on the present day that such a normal scenario appears so odd and unimaginable to us.

These are but leaps of imagination, and I do not pretend to anticipate the means which humanity and the chaos of free selection will use to create the order and stability we require to govern vital aspects of our society. They do also rely upon an assumption by business of a level of morality to which most leaders of industry would profess and perhaps aspire, but to which fewer adhere. While this might appear idealistic, it is far more realistic than hoping that this level of morality will ever develop in the thought or actions of the world's political leaders. The corporate world of today, however entwined with the state on some levels, is still largely dependent on the free will of billions of people and survives by supplying the products and services that we select. We have a choice.

31

Emptying the Corridors of Power

The author registered the One Less Party to field a candidate in the 1998 general election, and will incorporate some of that experience into this chapter.

> *The mystery of government is not how Washington works but how to make it stop.*
>
> P.J. O'Rourke, *Parliament of Whores*

The old adage goes: "Don't vote, it only encourages them." True, but many nation states now make voting a mandatory requirement, and those that do not will still assume the mantle of "the majority" when less than a quarter of the population have supposedly supported them with their mandate. I say supposedly, because the balance is nearly always tipped by people voting against someone else rather than in support of them. Many of today's non-voters do not vote because they are disgusted by the whole charade, but the system just counts them as apathetic, ignoring their non-vote. The system meanwhile just trundles on as if everything was going according to plan, and a working party is set up to find ways of getting more people to appreciate the "value" of their vote.

During the 1990s England's new breed of fluffy activists found ways to enmesh and embroil the state in its own convoluted laws and regulations, which it was breaking with regularity when dealing with protesters seeking to save the planet. Charges against them were frequently dropped soon after arrests were made. Perhaps there is a way to use the sacred "right" to vote itself as the tool with which we disempower the state. Perhaps there is a way to retract the people's mandate altogether. What would happen if there was a way to vote against the politicians themselves, rather than just picking one from the selection?

Well, I did have an idea on this some years ago, the memory of which was revived in the writing of this book. It arose as a result of a commitment I made to my politically eccentric friend Rainbow George one addled evening. Somehow he got me, a dedicated political de-activist, to agree to launch a political party of some sort at his next Rainbow Alliance press conference. There was a local by-election involved, and George kept phoning to remind me of my promise. I like to keep my commitments, even those that I wish I had never made.

As the event drew near, I put my mind to the problem one evening and drafted the skeleton of a platform for which it would seem worth casting a vote. It was named the No-Candidate Party, and I was "Gregory Sams—not standing for Parliament." There's a little double entendre here, playing on my status as a wheelchair user. I printed up a press release and cards with "political de-activist" printed under my name. It got a mention in a few newspapers and a radio interview but never went much further at the time.

Later, in the UK's June 2001 general election, I revived the idea and enlisted my friend Charlotte Regan to run as candidate for the re-named One Less Party. Charlotte is the daughter of the late Simon Regan, founder of the fearless and scandalous publication *Scallywag*.

The One Less Party had a legally binding Oath of Agreement, which every candidate is obliged to sign. The simple agreement went like this:

> *I undertake, if elected as a Member of Parliament (MP) at the forthcoming general election, never to attend a session of Parliament or vote on any issues whatsoever, nor partake in any parliamentary committees or fact-finding missions, nor in any way to perform any of the functions of office normally associated with being an MP. I further undertake never to encash any payments forthcoming as wages, salary, or remuneration for being an MP. I will never claim expenses, allowed or otherwise, for performance of functions I hereby swear not to perform. I will never employ or engage anybody on wages with regard to my position as an MP, be they relatives, friends, or total strangers. I guarantee that I will never mis-represent my constituents or "the people" or in any way attempt or pretend to represent them within the government and House of Commons. I will, effectively, do (or not do), everything possible in order to be simply one less politician.*

Each vote for the One Less Party is a vote for one less politician, sending shudders down the corridors of power, followed by a disturbing tremor should a single seat in Parliament be emptied in this way. It is a vote against all of the parties currently vying for control. It also stops anyone from assuming that you don't vote because you are too lazy or apathetic to take part in the exciting process of choosing a bunch of new faces to create yet more legislation and break their promises for the next however many years. The One Less Party concept seems an ideal complement to the Occupy movements of the early twenty-first century, providing a de-occupying balance at the other end of the spectrum.

This new party is not presented as some sort of ultimate technique for unraveling the state but as a simple and effective part of getting the process rolling—a catalyst and a spur to other more important and relevant action that is not even determinable at this time. It could well prompt the business and general community to initiate more construction of working alternatives to the 20 percent of the state's work that is essential to our society. One less politician is no big deal in itself, but if brought about by the vote and not a bullet or a bomb, then it would be something genuinely new in the political world, and a sign to its practitioners that they should begin looking for real jobs.

> *What politics is really about is a lot of mirrors and blue smoke. People have power when other people think they have power. If they don't think that, then you're an empty vessel.*
>
> Wyche Fowler, American politician, 1940–

There is no One Less Party in place at the time of writing, and this author hopefully casts the concept into the public arena. The structure is extremely simple and could in theory be applied anywhere in the world. I have no idea of how funding for deposits and whatever else would be obtained, and hope that anyone undertaking such an important venture would find a means to profit from its success, while not feeding upon the public purse.

Disclaimer: *For their own health and happiness, as well as ours, all readers are advised never to get mixed up in politics, and never to run for public office.*

32

And Where from Here?

The time is always right to do what is right.

Martin Luther King, Jr., 1929–1968

I do not mean to suggest that all our problems are caused by the state and its institutions, but I would suggest that most of them are. I also maintain that if we were neither financing these institutions nor suffering their inevitable negative side effects, we as a world community would eventually create the structures we need in order to live safe, healthy, and happy lives, sustainably. We are good at that sort of stuff, and better equipped when left in charge of the half or more or our created wealth that is siphoned off by the state through taxation and other mechanisms.

We do need structures as complex as the insurance industry or the airline industry, and they must in many cases be built from scratch. In the United Kingdom we already see society seeking to escape the state's failings in areas such as healthcare. This has led to the growth of an entire alternative industry offering therapies ranging from acupuncture to Bach Flower Remedies to remedial massage to Chinese herbalism. It is noteworthy that these new healing enterprises have thrived in a free market—despite the fact that their main competition, the National Health Service, is provided as a "free service" (paid for by taxation). Some of this new industry is now under sustained attack by the pharmaceutical and medical industry lobbies, seeking to re-establish the status quo by convincing the state that these alternative treatments are somehow dangerous to the public.

The generation before me had no concept of private security firms, today a global multi-billion dollar industry. The police were responsible for our personal and corporate security. But in the past five or six decades security firms have mushroomed across the world as the state becomes less able to protect us from robbery and attack, distracted by a legislative mountain of victimless crimes. South Africa alone boasts some nine thousand security firms, employing more personnel than the police and army. There and elsewhere, those who pay for the services of private security firms must continue to pay for the state's diminishing protection service. Imagine how much more we could achieve if we only had to pay once, and only for the service we want.

It will take an attitude change among more business leaders. We see this taking place already as increasing numbers of companies pay respect, and not just lip-service, to environmental and health concerns, taking positive action long before being required to do so by government legislation. They have friends, partners, and children too, with a public image that is often built on genuine foundations and not simply a desire to be voted back into power.

I optimistically put some trust in human nature—this because I have more often than not found the raw material to be worthy of that trust. I believe that when responsibility for morality is taken from the immoral state and returned to society, our society will be able to construct a means to recover its lost integrity, and engineer a return to safe environments needing fewer police and jails, not more. These police might come to be funded by the insurance industry, which can only profit from reduced levels of crime and hazards to the human race. Criminals who steal things don't get much use out of their plunder without a wide network of industries accepting their payments, whether restaurants, phone providers, shoe shops, or airlines. We will also need a means of exchange and a banking system that operates to the same moral standards as the rest of our human community. Until we suffer the consequences of letting a few of them go bust, we will never break the grip that criminally immoral bankers have upon our world. When we do, there will be space for moral banking and a stimulus for other exchange mediums such a Bitcoins and LETS.

There has been serious and worthwhile study of mechanisms in a genuinely free market that could deal with the seemingly intractable problems we would confront without a state. One example of this, which I touched upon, was how to deal effectively with coercive crimes in a non-coercive manner. This and many issues can be addressed, or naturally developed, though in many cases would be obstructed by the state's monopolistic control of the arena. In other instances, the enterprise structures needed to do the job might not fit into one of the specified business structures that are defined by legislation, and amenable to the tax authorities.

We can do it. More than ever before in human history, we have the technological tools and the intellect needed to advance our civilization into a sane and sustainable future. We will never be able to take this course, however, while still carrying the monkey of the state on our backs, diverting the resources that we have generated into ever more distorting and damaging schemes, hopeless programs, and deadly confrontations with other monkeys.

As I said in the beginning, this book isn't proposing a new way to run the world because there is no way to "run" such a complex system. In his satirical novel *1984*, George Orwell warned us of the possible future in an "ideal" Soviet world. Perhaps unwittingly, he came close to depicting the uniform society and permissible mindset to which many statesmen today would seem to aspire—albeit with a full refrigerator and high-speed Internet. It is now apparent, however, that it is beyond anybody's powers to accomplish such control, be they saint or Stalin, and that what we, humanity, are suffering from today is the result of the fumbling and dangerous attempts of the state to achieve its dream version of George Orwell's nightmare.

That which we most reliably enjoy today is the fruit of our own complex and chaotic society, not the creation of any parliament, king, pope, prophet, or emperor. We can live happily within our complex system, and we can find ways to govern and manage the more universal elements of it.

I can make but a few suggestions on how we regain our freedom from the state and correct or unravel the iniquities of history. This is a job for the complex system to resolve—for the freedom of billions to assemble from the bottom up. It is not a job suited to politicians, even those who say they will do all those things that we so want to happen. If we are to govern our human existence successfully, we must recognize that this cannot be done using coercion as the basic underlying tool. If we choose to attack the state and are successful, we then become the next state. Do not attack the state, nor depend on its tainted milk. Just live without it as a focus in your life and build to survive its inevitable decay.

Credits

In my own more than half century on this planet I have always sought the new and the unusual, often being exposed to and embracing ideas years, even decades before they began to assume a popular impact on the culture. This has not stopped me, ever, from appreciating the old and traditional—though not for the sake of it being old or traditional. I have, during this time, studied how new ideas emerge and penetrate the culture, often helping with the process.

Though life itself is the ultimate teacher, the main signposts have been indicated to me by Lao Tzu, Charles Fort, Georges Ohsawa, Professor Galambos, and the findings of the early workers in chaos theory such as Benoit Mandelbrot, Ralph Abraham, and Edward Lorenz. These great men's ideas have been assimilated with those of my forward-thinking parents and countless other teachers, pioneers, and friends, then tested against my observations of life and our society on the planet.

Charles Fort made me realize that many events in the world are unexplained by any known science or thought system, and that serendipity and coincidence are not nearly as random as one would have thought. He was my first exposure to the notion of the "Butterfly Effect," though I hardly absorbed it from his obtuse example, which ran something like "Not a bottle of ketchup shall fall from a tenement window in New York that will not affect the price of rice in China."

Georges Ohsawa taught me about self-responsibility and the importance of food in our lives. He taught me that food was anything consumed through the mouth, eyes, ears, or other senses. My brother had introduced me to his ideas, and our focus for many years thereafter was the food we put in our mouths. Our ability to do so was greatly enhanced by the natural food upbringing our parents, Kenneth (*www.ultimateflyingobject.co.uk*) and Margaret, gave us. This led to the introduction of many natural foods to the British diet from 1967 and eventually to my launching of the original "all natural—all vegetable" VegeBurger in 1982, with a few other "firsts" in between. My understanding of self-responsibility at an early age was also immensely helpful in dealing with life from a wheelchair, after breaking my back in 1966 at the age of eighteen.

Professor Galambos' lessons made me realize that we would not, as a society, be able to eat our way out of the problems that face us. He alerted me to the basic failings of coercion as a tool of government and taught me about the profitability of morality and the morality of profitability. His definition of profit is "any increase in happiness obtained through moral action." I discovered that right wing and left wing are but different tilts of the same bird. Galambos in particular figured out coercion-free mechanisms that could successfully be run by us as a society, in order to manage the areas that the state has monopolized for many years. He taught me about the Wright Brothers and how insurance works. He also made me realize how much I had to gain by fully appreciating the value to me of the ideas of men who explored new thought, men such as Lao Tzu, Archimedes, Giordano Bruno, Galileo Galilei, Isaac Newton, Thomas Paine, and Nicola Tesla. Though almost unheard of today, Andrew J. Galambos belongs in this select group.

Discovering chaos theory in 1990 brought together all the currents of my life to date—and introduced me to one of the greatest principles of this Universe. It made immediate sense of all life's wonderful synergy when I recognized that it was the nature of the Universe to create harmony and beauty. I rapidly perceived the significance of the discoveries of chaos theory to our society and saw how we thwart the constructive energies of chaos by seeking to forcibly govern it. I wanted to make sure that these discoveries would not remain in the province of the hard sciences and would be recognized as operating in our society as well as the rest of the Universe. I opened Strange Attractions, the world's first shop dedicated to chaos theory, passing it into the hands of one Thornton Streeter after three years. For a few years after that I pursued the path of a successful fractographer and artist, responsible for hundreds of thousands of fractally decorated posters, cards, mugs, jigsaw puzzles, and other products, as well as for literally tens of millions of imprints licensed to magazines and publications around the world.

It is my hope that concepts like the "Butterfly Effect" of chaos theory will have fluttered sufficiently into the popular culture for this book to land upon receptive ears. We have lost much progress following in the failed footsteps of the past. If we are to survive and prosper into the future, it will be when we take responsibility for that future ourselves.

Big Butterflies

A few names stand out of the seamless passage of chaos—people who triggered important changes in my life, sometimes through simple contributions.

Special thanks to the late Dr. Nakadadi, who set my mother and father on the wholefood path in the late 1940s, and to them for keeping to it. Thanks especially to my brother Craig, who in 1966 brought macrobiotics to the UK and to my attention. His interest was triggered when the books of Georges Ohsawa were seized and burnt by the FBI—because Ohsawa suggested that the "all-American" diet of red meat, white starches, and fizzy drinks was a tad dangerous.

For the introduction to A.J. Galambos' unique courses, I must thank John Fountain, Evan R. Soulé, and Kim Bockus, who between them provided the stimulus and material.

During the VegeBurger days, some great leaps forward were made through a lunch with Annette Middleton, a pint or two with Lindsay Vincent, and much time in the company of the always amazing Mister Larry Switzer.

My immersion into chaos theory was prompted by artist Howie Cooke, and developed through my interactions with Peter Cox, Ernie, Filiz, Grant, and Jesse Jones, who wrote the excellent fractal software called Mandella (also Mandelbrowser).

Thanks too in the inspirations department to Susannah, Martyn, Phoenix, George, Des Kay, and their tribes: to Jeff, Hoppy, Sue, Raja Ram, and Bonnie for their part in many personal transformations; to my former wife Sandy for her tireless support over the years; to Sterling for his thorough rough draft review; to James for his relentless proofreading, to SchNEWS for the disclaimer style, and to the many friends and associates who have supported and encouraged my activities through the years.

Resources

A few authors whose books have influenced ideas raised in this book:

Briggs, John and Peat, David F., *Turbulent Mirror*. New York: Harper & Rowe, 1990.

Bryson, Bill. *Made in America*. London: Secker & Warburg Ltd., 1994.

Capra, Fritjof. *The Web of Life*. London: HarperCollins, 1996.

Carson, Rachel. *Silent Spring*. London: Hamish Hamilton, 1963.

Cheney, Margaret. *Tesla: Man Out of Time*. London: Prentice Hall Int. Inc., 1981.

Davies, Paul. *God and the New Physics*. London: Penguin Books Ltd., 1983.

Drexler, Eric. *Engines of Creation*. New York: Anchor, 1987.

Duncan, Alan and Hobson, Dominic. *Saturn's Children*. London: Sinclair-Stevenson, 1995.

Ehrenreich, Barbara. *Blood Rites*. London: Virago Press, 1997.

Fishall, R.T. *Bureaucrats: How to Annoy Them*. London: Arrow Books Ltd., 1981.

Garcia, Linda. *The Fractal Explorer*. Santa Cruz, CA: Dynamic Press, 1991.

Gleick, James. *Chaos*. London: William Heinemann Ltd., 1988.

Goldsmith, James. *The Trap.* London: Macmillan Ltd., 1994.

Hauschka, Rudolf. *Nutrition.* London: Rudolf Steiner Press, 1967.

Hofstadter, Douglas R. *Gödel, Escher, Bach.* Great Britain, Harvester, 1979.

Huxley, Aldous. *The Doors of Perception and Heaven and Hell.* London: HarperCollins, 1990.

Leary, Timothy. *Chaos and Cyberculture.* Berkeley, CA: Ronin Publishing, 1994.

McKenna, Terence. *Food of the Gods.* London: Rider, Random House, 1992.

Merrick. *Battle for the Trees.* Leeds: Godhaven Ink, 1996.

Murray, William. *Anarchic Harmony.* Port Townsend, WA: Loompanics, 1992.

Ohsawa, George. *Zen Macrobiotics.* Los Angeles: Ohsawa Foundation Inc., 1965.

Orwell, George. *1984.* London: Penguin Books Ltd., 1949.

Paine, Thomas. *Common Sense and the Crisis.* New York: Anchor Press, 1973.

Pauwels, Louis and Bergier, Jacques. *The Morning of the Magicians.* London: Anthony Gibbs and Phillips Ltd., 1963.

Prigogine, Ilya and Stengers, Isabelle. *Order Out of Chaos.* London: Flamingo, Fontana Paperbacks, 1985.

Rand, Ayn. *Atlas Shrugged and The Fountain Head.* Great Britain: Cassell & Co Ltd., 1947.

Schwenk, Theodor. *Sensitive Chaos.* London: Rudolf Steiner Press, 1965.

Stewart, Ian. *Does God Play Dice?* London: Penguin Books Ltd., 1990.

Tsu, Lao. *Tao Te Ching.* New York: Random House Inc., 1972.

Thoreau, Henry David. *Walden Pond, or Life in the Woods.* Boston: Ticknor and Fields, 1854.

Watson, Lyall. *Supernature.* London: Coronet, Hodder & Stoughton Ltd., 1973.

Watts, Alan. *The Book: On the Taboo Against Knowing Who You Are.* New York: Random House, 1966.

Wong, Eva. *The Shambhala Guide to Taoism.* Boston & London: Shambhala, 1997.

The Golden Rule

Christianity:
All things whatsoever you would that men should do to you, do ye even so to them: for this is the Law and the Prophets.
Matthew, 7.12

Judaism:
What is hateful to you, do not do to your fellow man. That is the entire Law; All the rest is commentary.
Talmud, Shabbet, 31a

Islam:
No one of you is a believer until he desires for his brother that which he desires for himself.
Sunnah

Brahmanism:
This is the sum of duty: Do naught unto others which would cause you pain if done to you.
Mahabarata, 51 1517

Buddhism
Hurt not others in ways that you yourself would find hurtful.
Udan-Varga, 5,18

Confucianism

Surely it is the maxim of loving kindness: Do not unto others that you would not have them do unto you.

Analects, 15.23

Taoism

Regard your neighbour's gain as your own gain, and your neighbour's loss as your own loss.

T'ai Shang Kan Ying Pien

Zoroastrianism

That nature alone is good which refrains from doing another whatsoever is not good for itself.

Dadistan-i-dinik, 94,5

- Note the difference between the Golden Rule's expression by Christianity or Islam and the other religions— the simple distinction between action and non-action.

- In Islam, your "brother" typically refers to fellow Muslims.

About the Author

Gregory Sams is a pioneer of food for the body and food for the mind. With his brother Craig, he co-founded Seed restaurant, the first natural and organic eatery in the UK, followed by Ceres Grain Store on Portobello Road, which catered to people who wanted to cook natural food at home. He then went on to create the all-organic brand Whole Earth food. At age 18, Greg founded *Harmony Magazine*, to which John Lennon dedicated an 8-frame cartoon. He later co-published *Seed: The Journal of Organic Living*. He lives in London. Author website: *www.gregorysams.com*